beholden

beholden

a poem as long as the river

rita wong & fred wah

talonbooks

beholden: a poem as long as the river arises out of a larger project titled *River Relations: A Beholder's Share of the Columbia River*, a collaboration of artists seeking a creative engagement with the Columbia River.

River Relations has been supported by the Social Sciences and Humanities Research Council of Canada and the Emily Carr University of Art and Design. Members of the project team, from different practices, have travelled and researched the River for several years – see www.riverrelations.ca.

The poem, represented along a 114-foot banner of the entire Columbia River, has been exhibited as part of a number of gallery presentations displayed in the Pacific Northwest.

Listen – on my way to get a pail of water down by the creek buhdum,

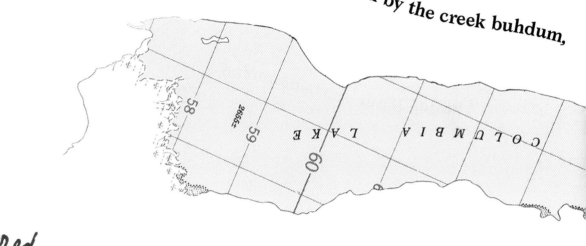

sacred starts here & water fills eyes, simply, honour

buhdum, Columbia River starts humming its invisible Kootenay qi path breathing what exists through itself is called as is meaning

say the names: Ktunaxa,

Pakisǫ́nuk (Columbia Lake First Nation), Kenpésǫt (Shuswap Band)

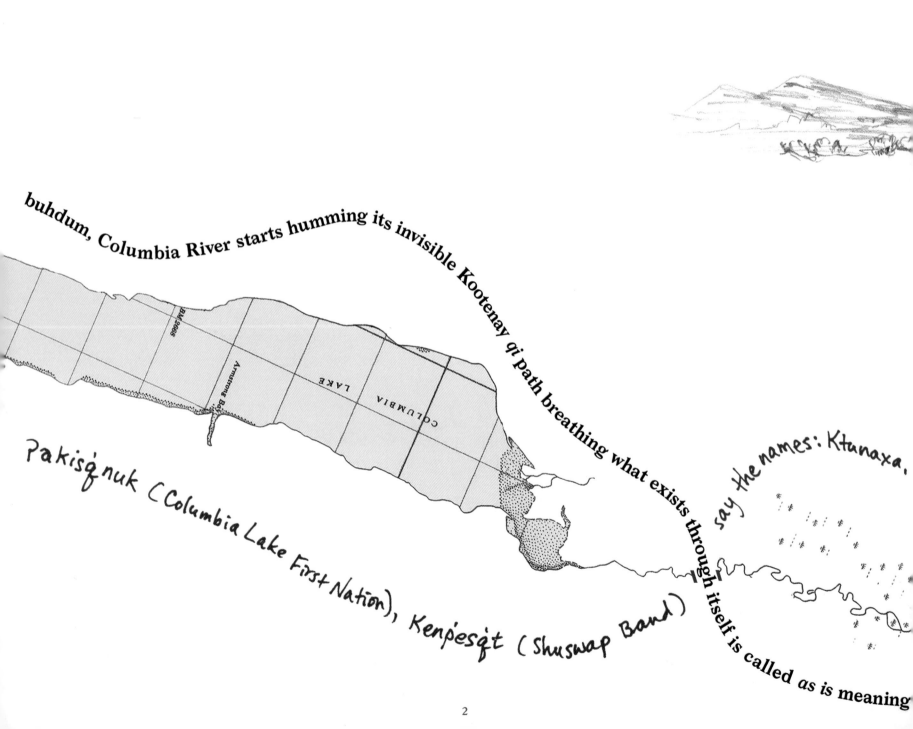

COLUMBIA LAKE

Armstrong Bay

BM 2668

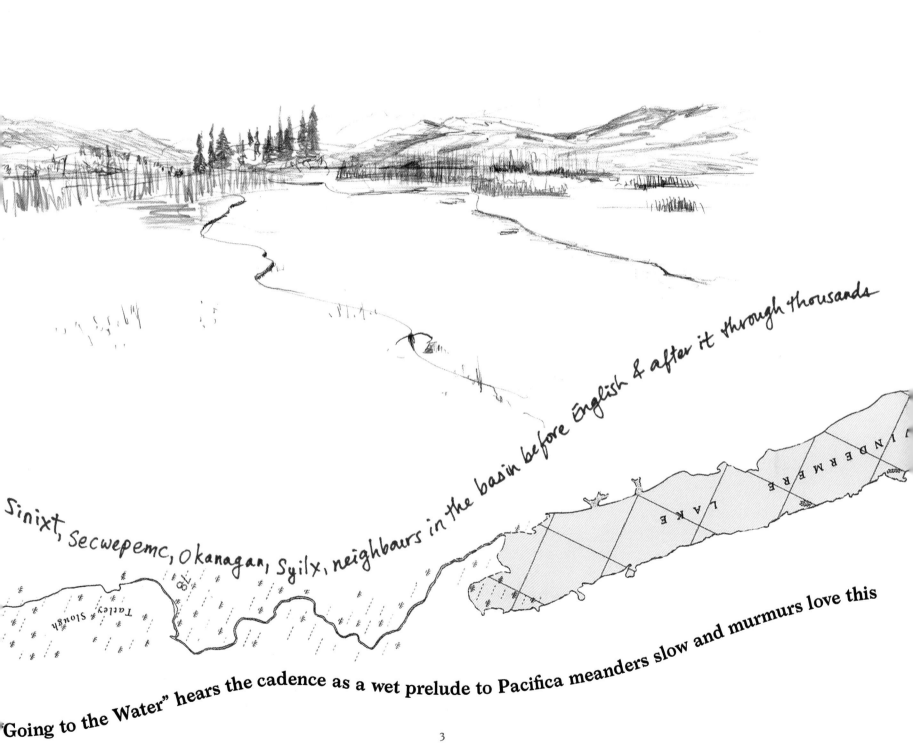

Sinixt, Secwepemc, Okanagan, Syilx, neighbours in the basin before English & after it through thousands

"Going to the Water" hears the cadence as a wet prelude to Pacifica meanders slow and murmurs love this

Tarley Slough

WINDERMERE LAKE

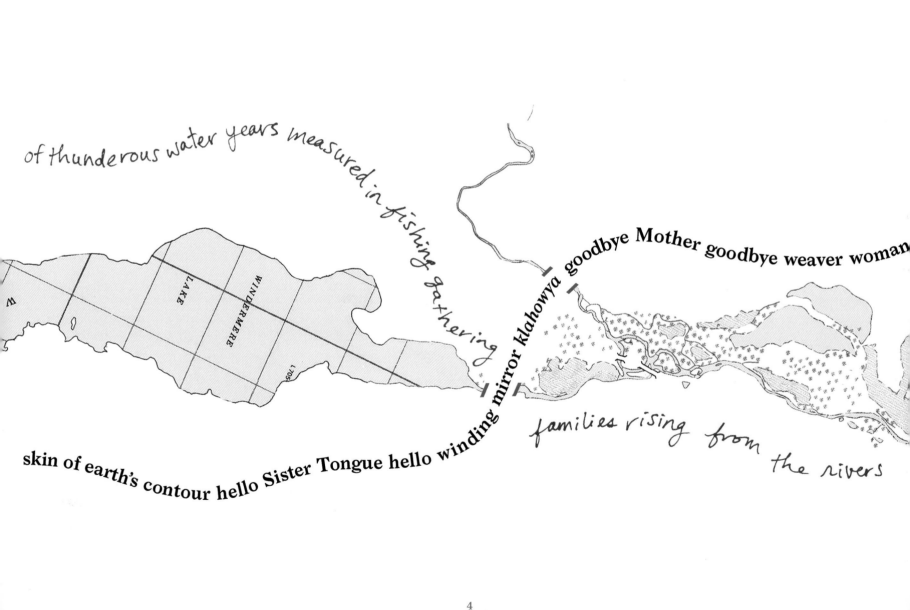

of thunderous water years measured in fishing gathering

skin of earth's contour hello Sister Tongue hello winding mirror klahowya goodbye Mother goodbye weaver woman

families rising from the rivers

LAKE WINDERMERE

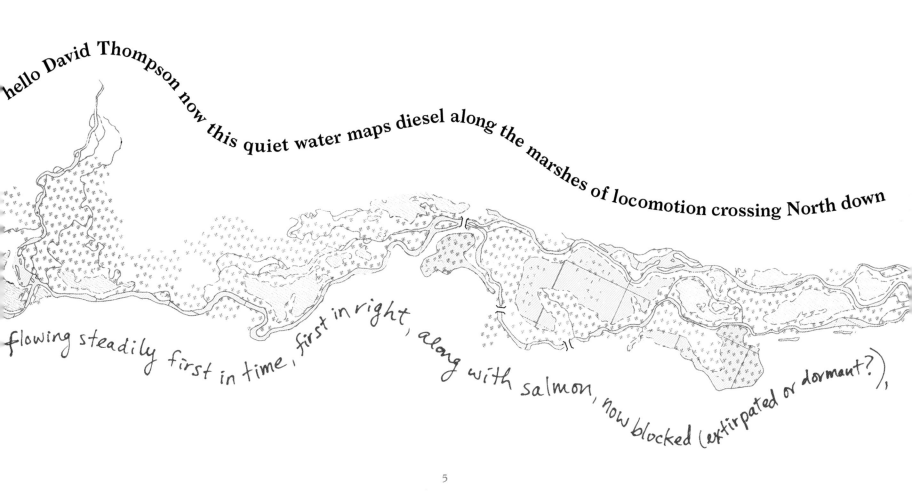

hello David Thompson now this quiet water maps diesel along the marshes of locomotion crossing North down

flowing steadily first in time, first in right, along with salmon, now blocked (extirpated or dormant?), the map of the River of Heaven Steamboat Mountain are you worried about a future – Nowitka truly every

bull trout, kokanee, pikeminnow, meandering through the river's kidneys, wuʔu cleansed by

6

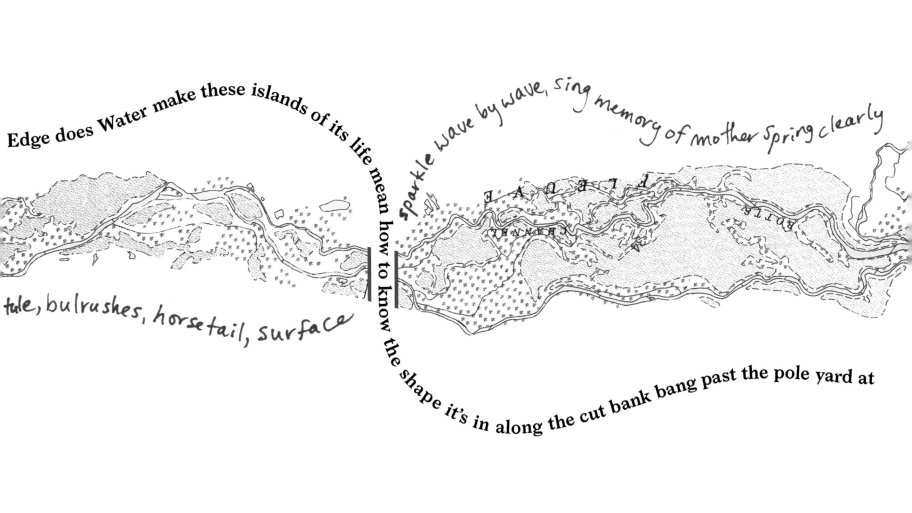

Edge does Water make these islands of its life mean how to know

sparkle wave by wave, sing memory of mother spring clearly

tule, bulrushes, horsetail, surface

the shape it's in along the cut bank bang past the pole yard at

reflecting clouds, sun, stars, all modes of creation, stirred by wind carrying mountain strength, sung

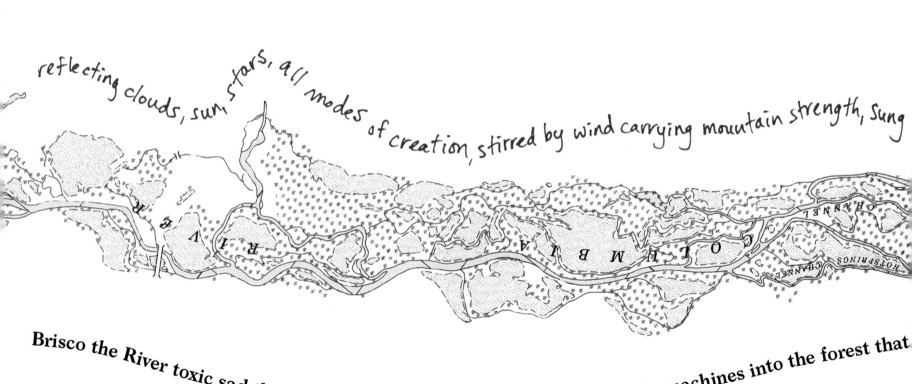

Brisco the River toxic sad those treated poles are not canoes spilling their machines into the forest that

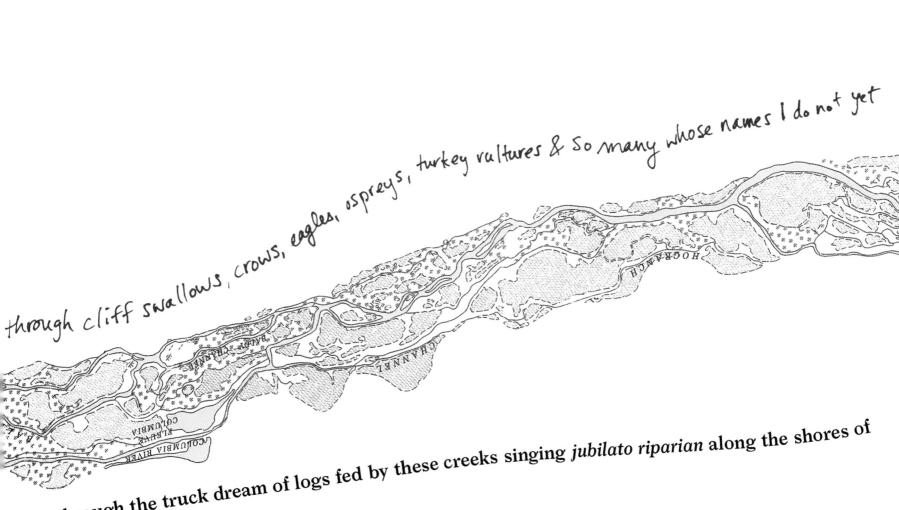

through cliff swallows, crows, eagles, ospreys, turkey vultures & so many whose names I do not yet

floats through the truck dream of logs fed by these creeks singing *jubilato riparian* along the shores of

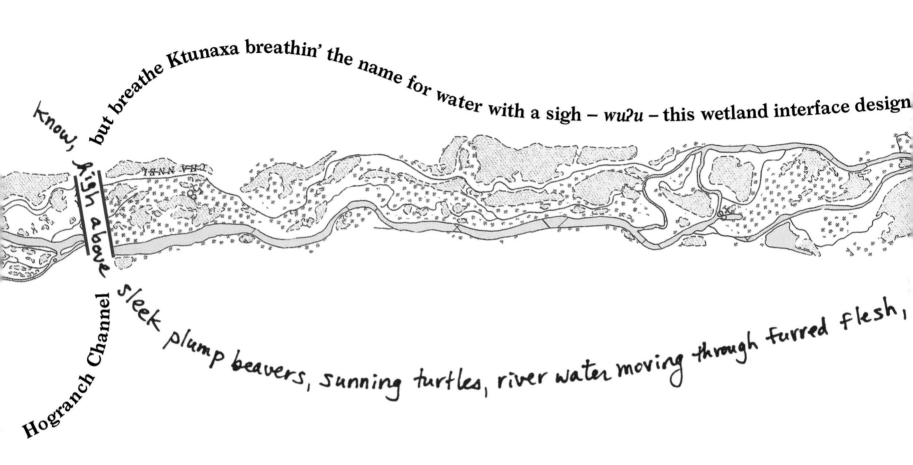

know, but breathe Ktunaxa breathin' the name for water with a sigh – *wuʔu* – this wetland interface design

sigh above

Hogranch Channel

sleek plump beavers, sunning turtles, river water moving through furred flesh,

of shrubs and grasses long harrowed trough that sleeps through Rocky Mountain Trench hello Horse Creek

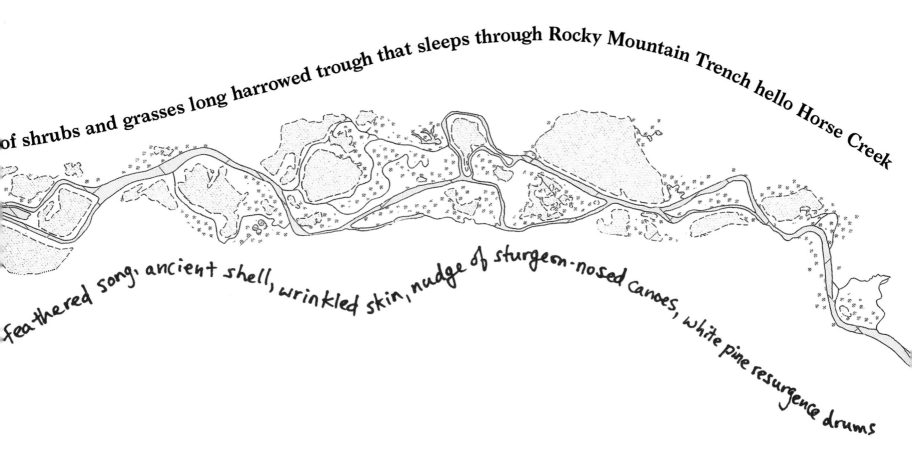

feathered song, ancient shell, wrinkled skin, nudge of sturgeon-nosed canoes, white pine resurgence drums

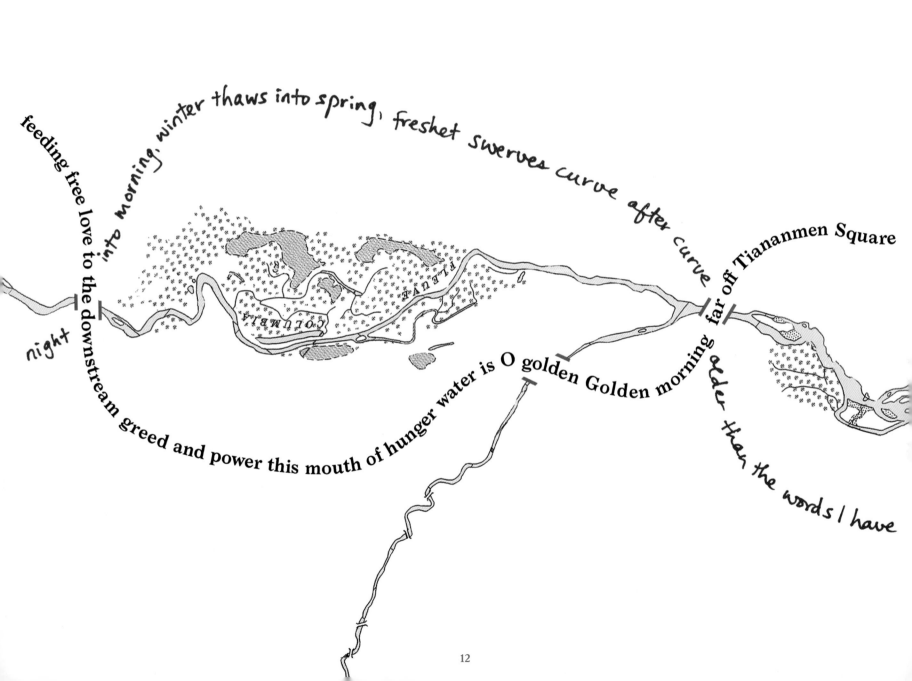

feeding free love to the downstream greed and power this mouth of hunger water is O golden Golden morning

into morning, winter thaws into spring, freshet swerves curve after curve

far off Tiananmen Square older than the words I have

night

COLUMBIA

FLEUVE

12

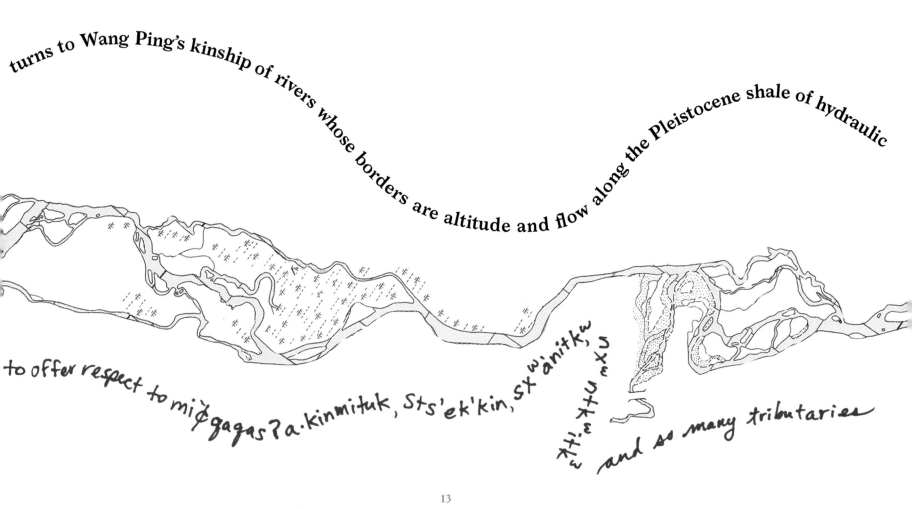

turns to Wang Ping's kinship of rivers whose borders are altitude and flow along the Pleistocene shale of hydraulic

to offer respect to miłqaqas ʔa·kinmituk, Sts'ek'kin, sx̌ʷənitkʷ, mxʷiˑłˑxʷumxʷ and so many tributaries

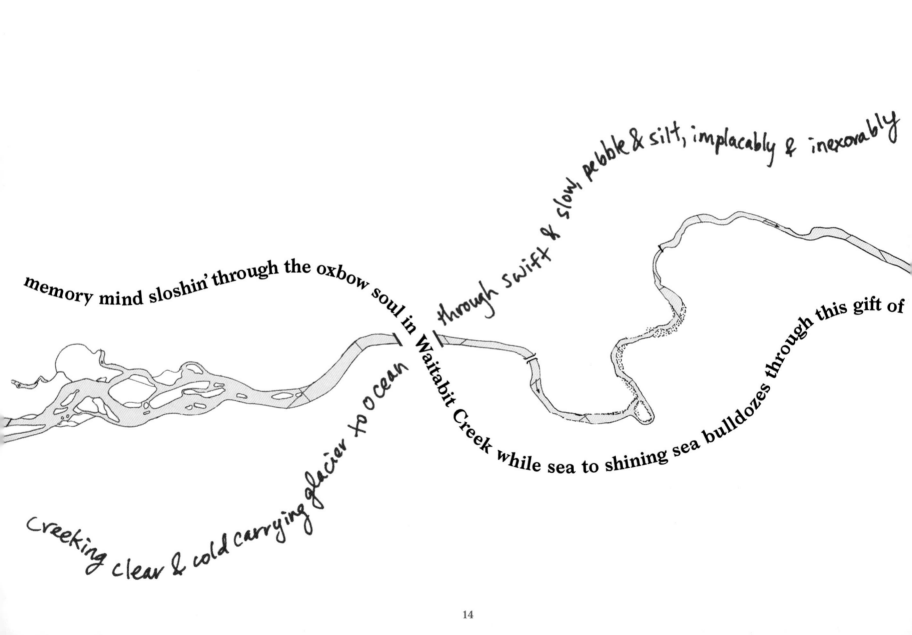

memory mind sloshin' through the oxbow soul in Waitabit Creek

through swift & slow, pebble & silt, implacably & inexorably

creeking clear & cold carrying glacier to ocean

while sea to shining sea bulldozes through this gift of

14

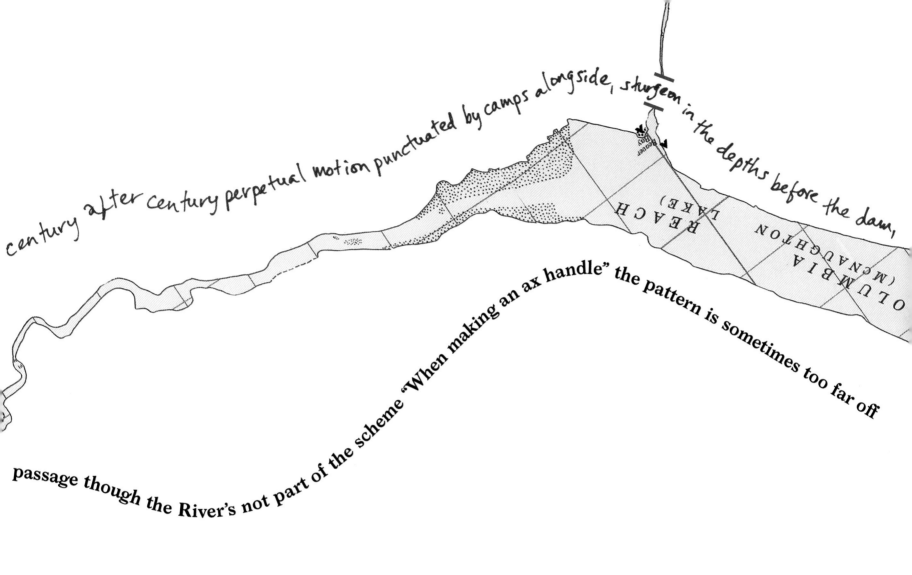

century after century perpetual motion punctuated by camps alongside, sturgeon in the depths before the dam,

COLUMBIA (McNAUGHTON) REACH LAKE

Becquet Buoy

passage though the River's not part of the scheme "When making an ax handle" the pattern is sometimes too far off

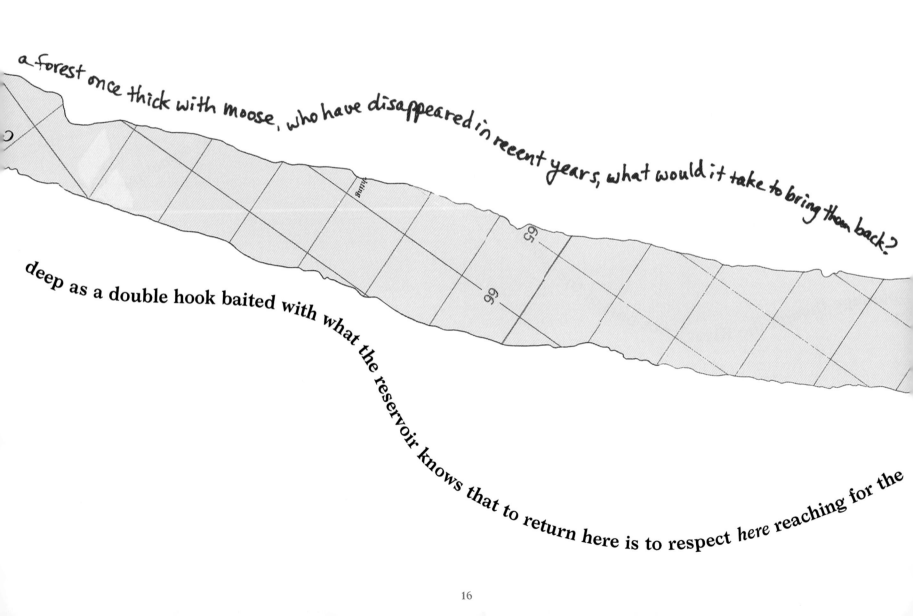

a forest once thick with moose, who have disappeared in recent years, what would it take to bring them back?

deep as a double hook baited with what the reservoir knows that to return here is to respect here reaching for the

Words pile up like a log jam, dam debris, riprap, trouble brewing like a slow-moving trainwreck, signalling maps are right language sshh so don't say a word our ancestors didn't forget us after

COLUMBIA
(McNAUGHTON)
REACH
(LAKE)

Esplanade Bay

Maximum 247'± Minimum 2320'±

Maximum 247'± Minimum 2320'±

29
30
31
32
33
34

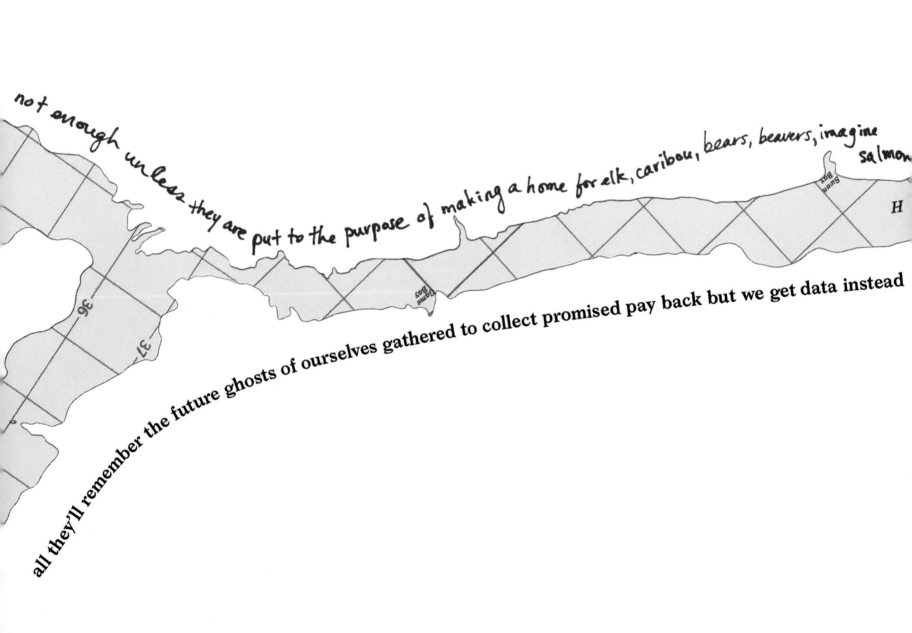

not enough unless they are put to the purpose of making a home for elk, caribou, bears, beavers, imagine salmon

all they'll remember the future ghosts of ourselves gathered to collect promised pay back but we get data instead

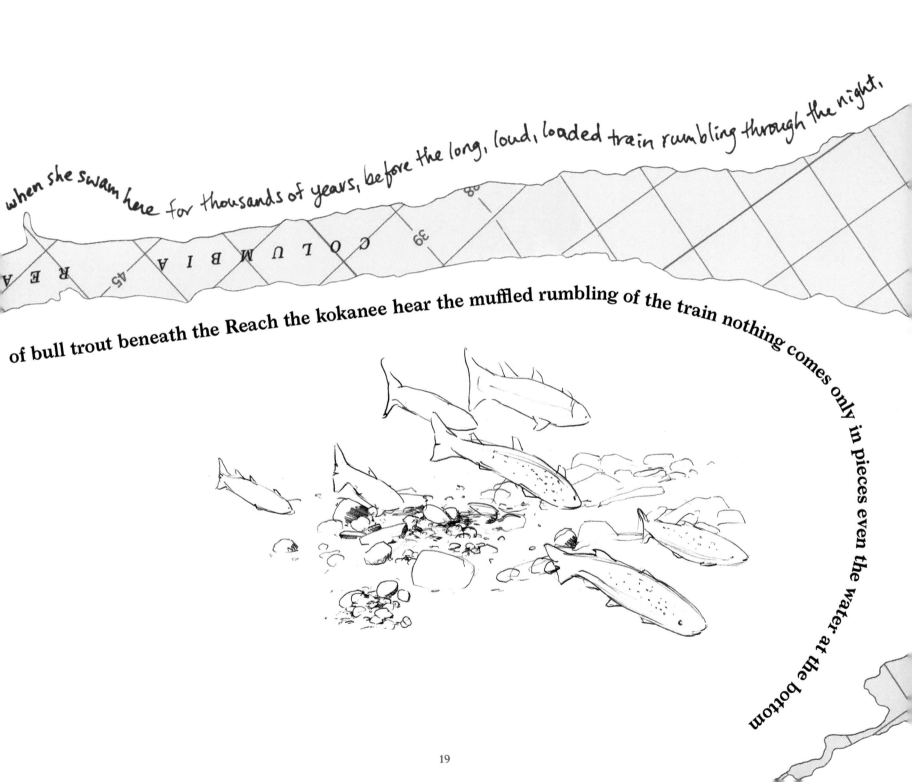

when she swam here for thousands of years, before the long, loud, loaded train rumbling through the night,

COLUMBIA REA
39 45 80

of bull trout beneath the Reach the kokanee hear the muffled rumbling of the train nothing comes only in pieces even the water at the bottom

carrying its deadly freight on schedule for the demon of speed chugging track by track, endless till it's not.

of this reservoir won't inundate the Secwepemc with that Big Bend thirst how to explain the irony of this adamantine

Windy Arm

Maximum 2477±
Minimum 2320±

Max 2475±
Min 2320±

L1433

COLUMBIA REACH
(McNAUGHTON LAKE)

Kinbasket Arm

SULLIVAN ARM

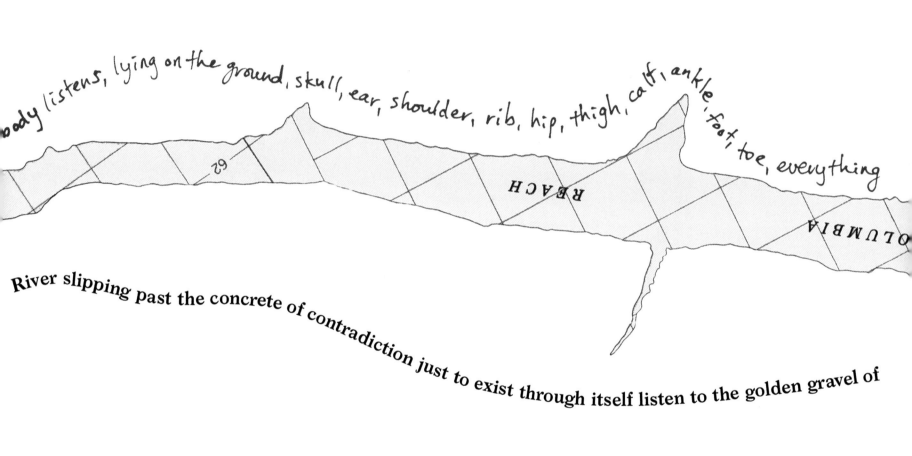

body listens, lying on the ground, skull, ear, shoulder, rib, hip, thigh, calf, ankle, foot, toe, everything

62

REACH

OLUMBIA

River slipping past the concrete of contradiction just to exist through itself listen to the golden gravel of

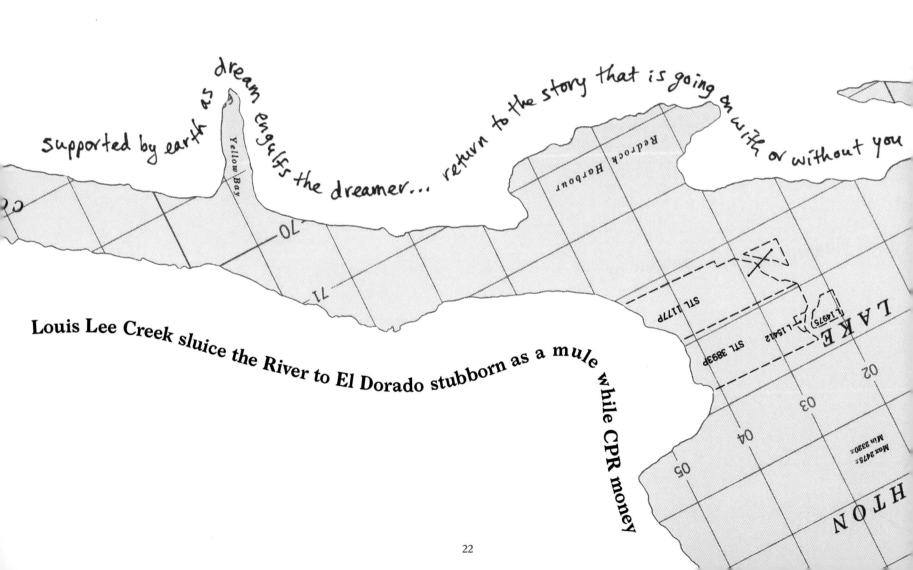

supported by earth as dream engulfs the dreamer... return to the story that is going on with or without you

Louis Lee Creek sluice the River to El Dorado stubborn as a mule while CPR money

Yellow Bay

Redrock Harbour

LAKE

70

71

STL 1117P

STL 1154I2

TL 14975

TL 15412

STL 3893P

02

03

04

05

Max 2475±
Min 2330±

HTON

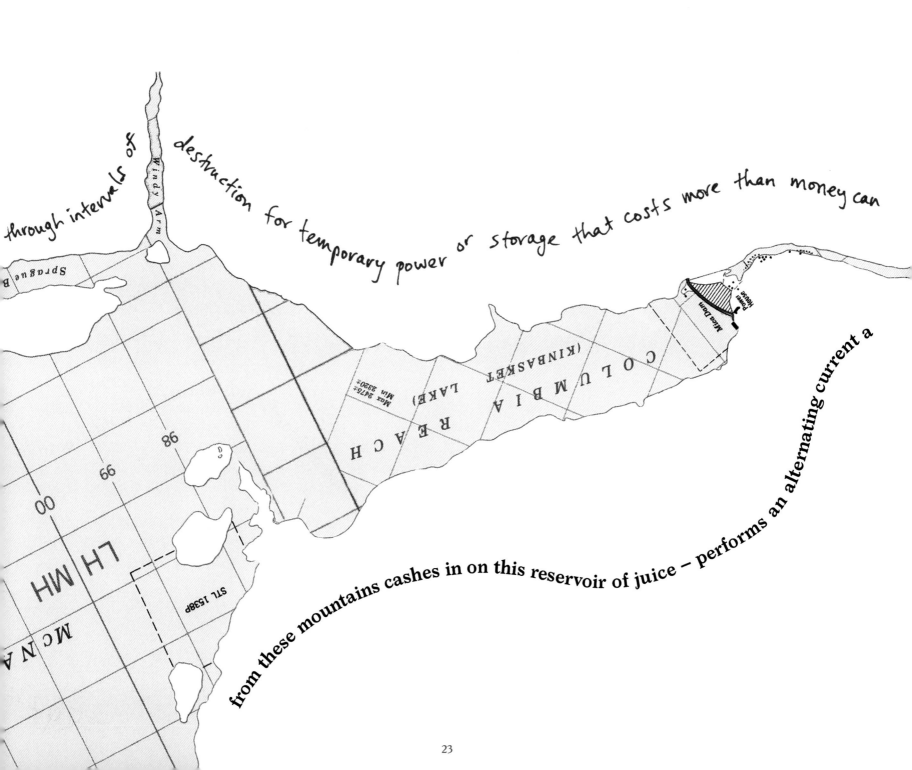

through intervals of destruction for temporary power or storage that costs more than money can

from these mountains cashes in on this reservoir of juice – performs an alternating current a

Windy Arm

Sprague

COLUMBIA REACH (KINBASKET LAKE)

Max 2475± Min 2350±

Mica Dam

Power House

MW LH

McNA

00

66

86

STL 1538P

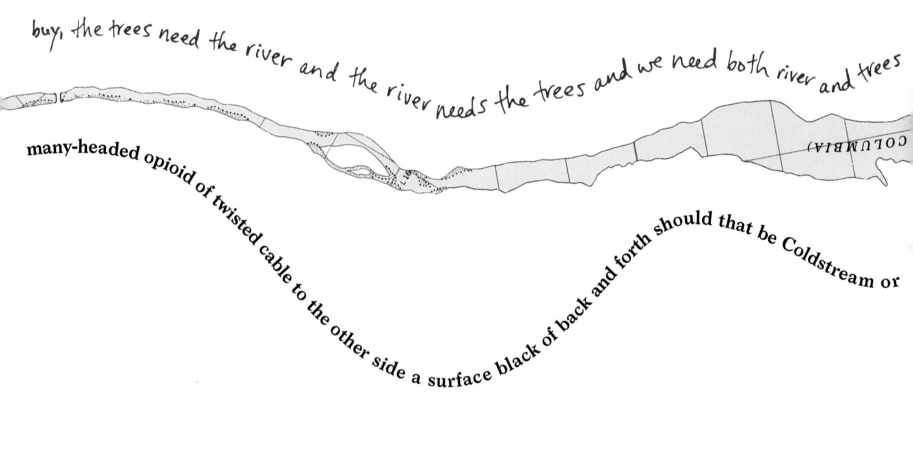

buy, the trees need the river and the river needs the trees and we need both river and trees

many-headed opioid of twisted cable to the other side a surface black of back and forth should that be Coldstream or

COLUMBIA)

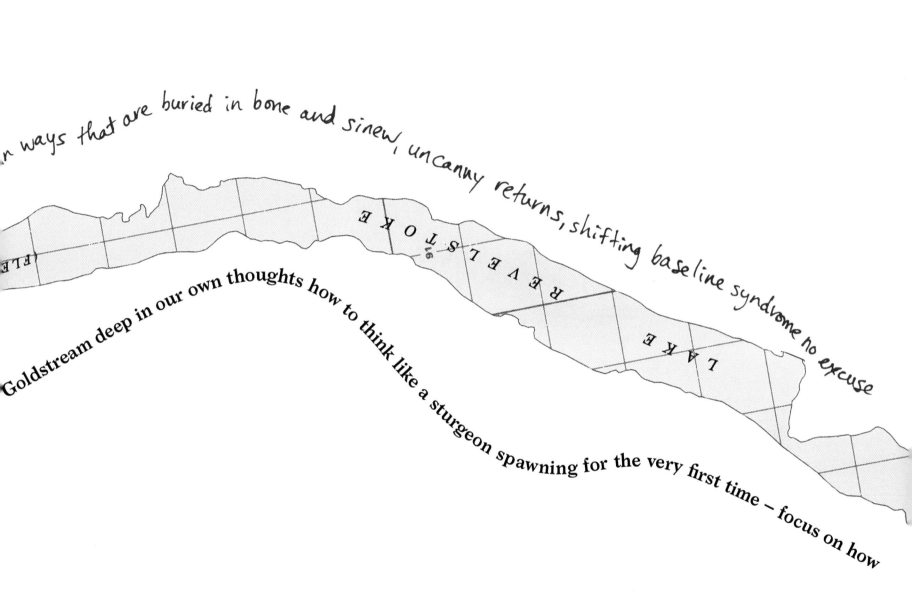

...n ways that are buried in bone and sinew, uncanny returns, shifting baseline syndrome no excuse

Goldstream deep in our own thoughts how to think like a sturgeon spawning for the very first time – focus on how

REVELSTOKE

LAKE

(FLE...)

for not learning the cultures of this land, better late than never to not take abundance

(COLUMBIA RIVER)   (COLUMBIA

39   38   37   3   4

breathing holds the heart for that loud Pacific tide you won't forget downstream there's gratitude in those over-

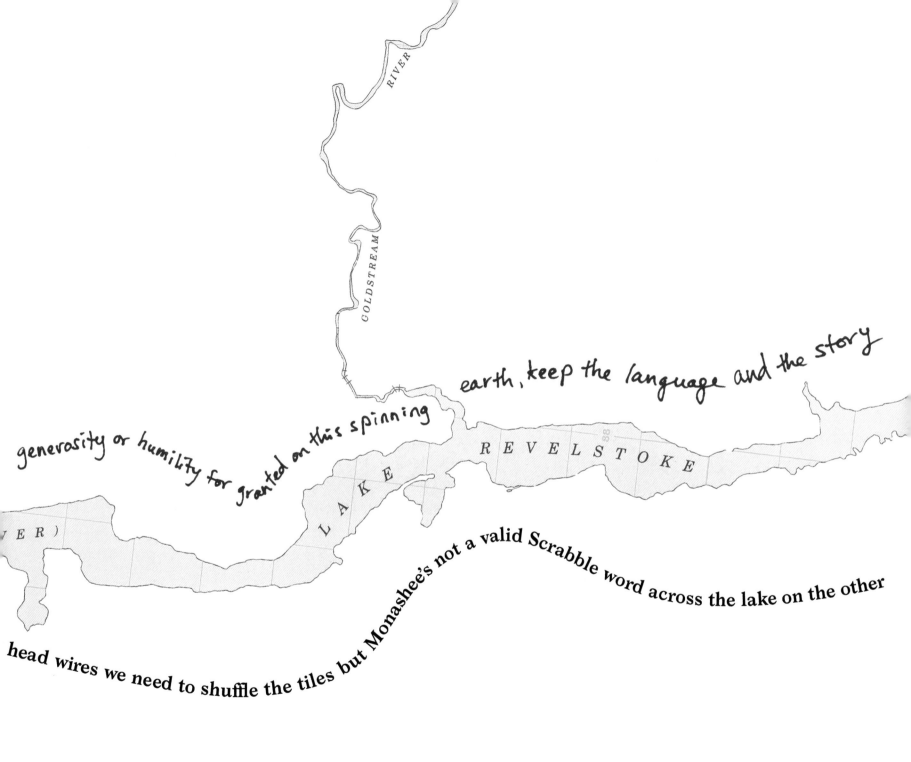

generosity or humility for granted on this spinning earth, keep the language and the story

head wires we need to shuffle the tiles but Monashee's not a valid Scrabble word across the lake on the other

RIVER

GOLDSTREAM

LAKE REVELSTOKE

ER)

honest, don't call a reservoir a lake... don't naturalize the hubris, don't hide the arrogance

(F L E U V E C O L U M B I A)

shore Site C marches on watching for a period at the end of this floating sentence how do you ask the River the

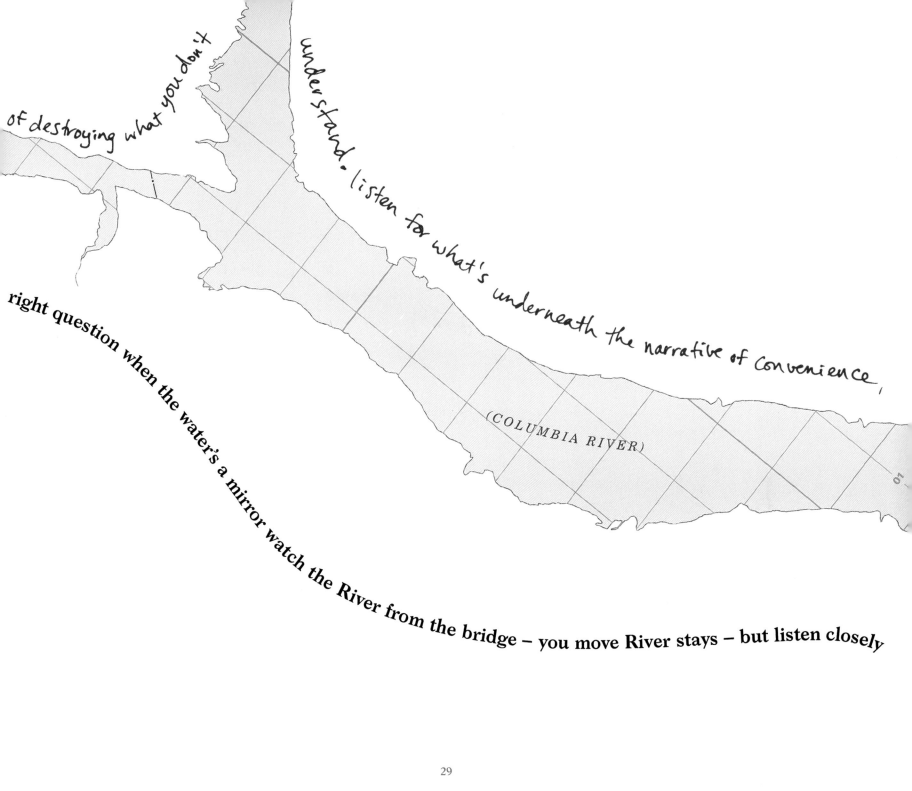

of destroying what you don't understand. listen for what's underneath the narrative of convenience,

right question when the water's a mirror watch the River from the bridge – you move River stays – but listen closely

(COLUMBIA RIVER)

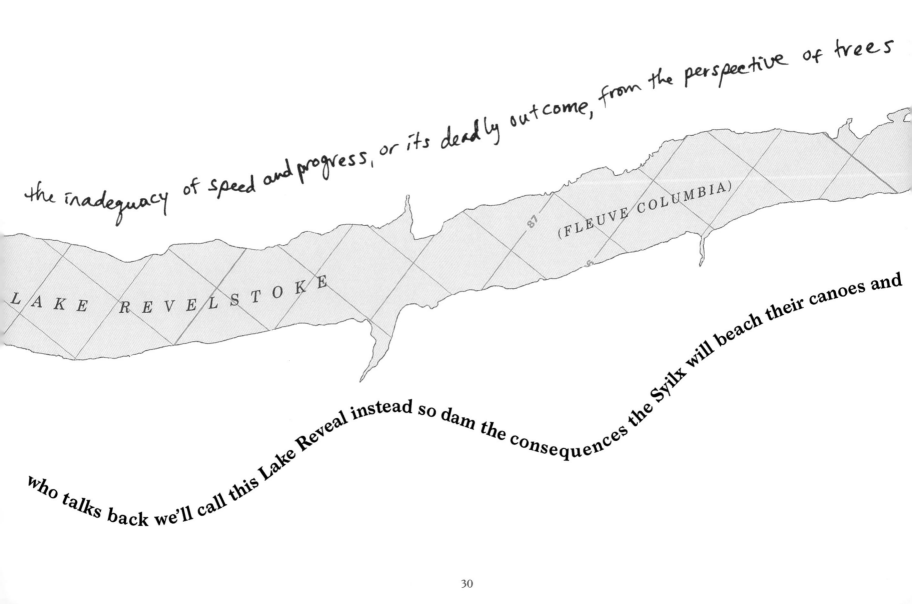

the inadequacy of speed and progress, or its deadly outcome, from the perspective of trees

(FLEUVE COLUMBIA)

87

LAKE REVELSTOKE

who talks back we'll call this Lake Reveal instead so dam the consequences the Syilx will beach their canoes and

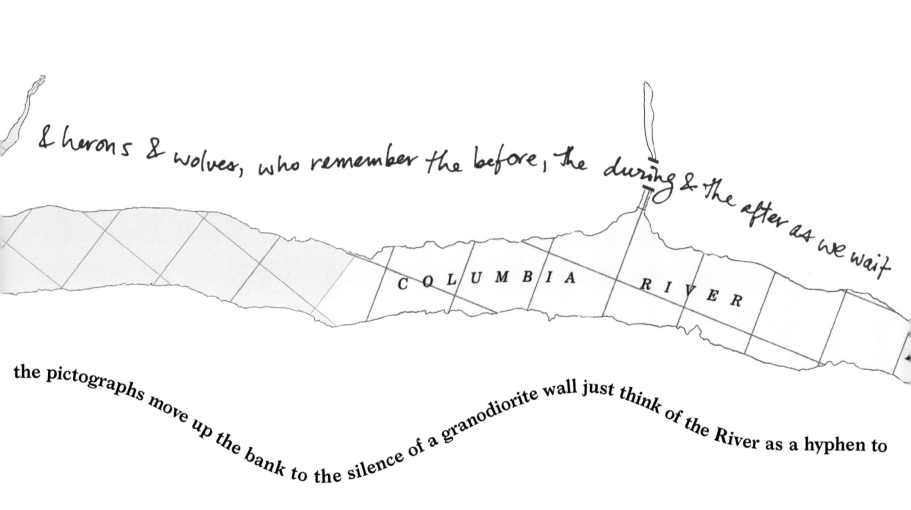

& herons & wolves, who remember the before, the during & the after as we wait

C O L U M B I A   R I V E R

the pictographs move up the bank to the silence of a granodiorite wall just think of the River as a hyphen to

for the leap to take hold or for the machinery of greed to dig a mass grave for

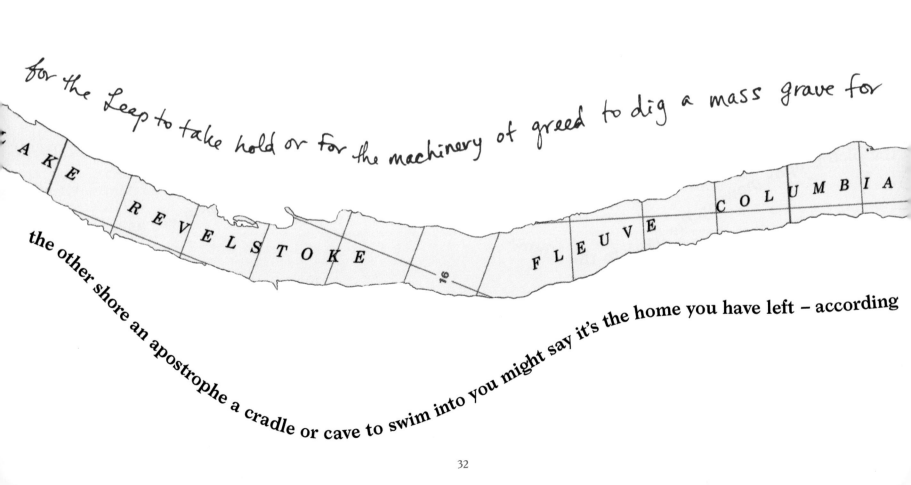

AKE REVELSTOKE 76 FLEUVE COLUMBIA

the other shore an apostrophe a cradle or cave to swim into you might say it's the home you have left – according

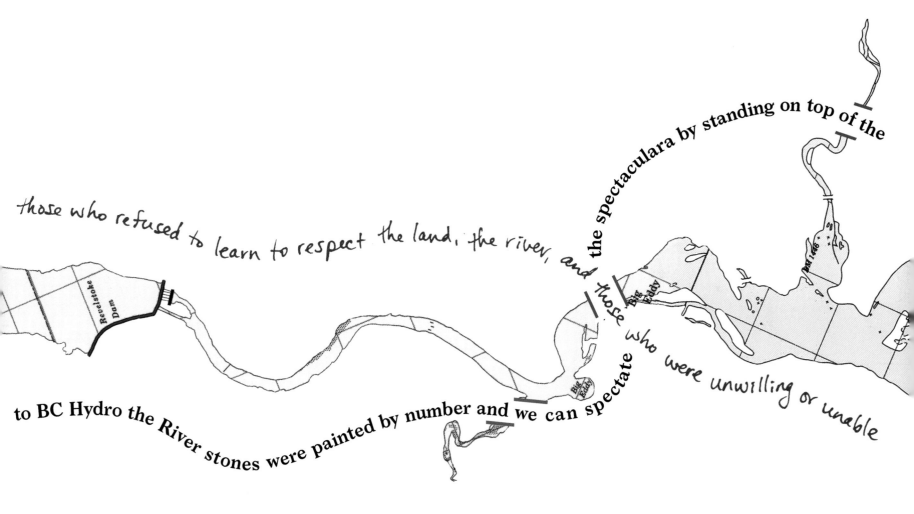

those who refused to learn to respect the land, the river, and the spectaculara by standing on top of the

to BC Hydro the River stones were painted by number and we can spectate

those who were unwilling or unable

Revelstoke Dam

Big Eddy

Big Eddy

powerhouse over the visitor centre whose house and who's home now Big Eddy says to the logger who thinks

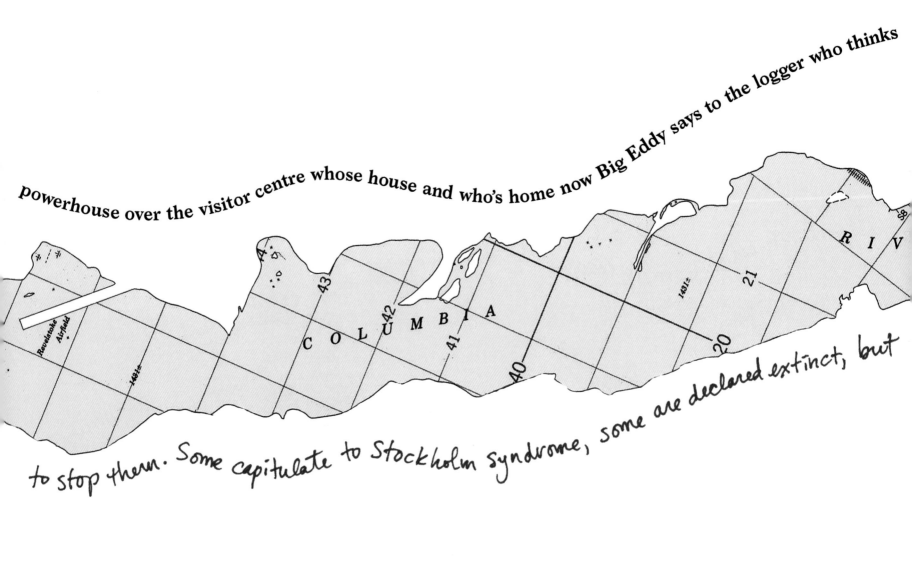

to stop them. Some capitulate to Stockholm syndrome, some are declared extinct, but

from the heart "Become like water my friend" now heading home I want to shout hello Grampa goodbye cable

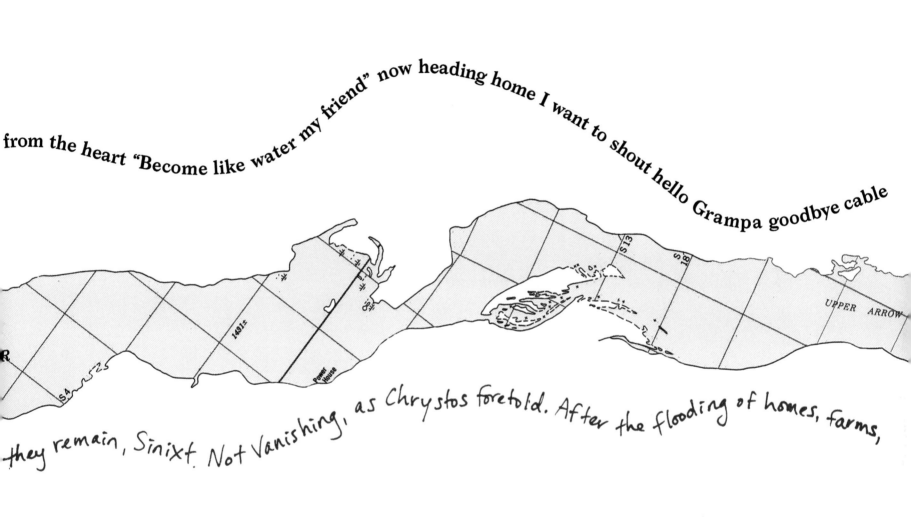

they remain, Sinixt. Not Vanishing, as Chrystos foretold. After the flooding of homes, farms,

ferry thanks for this name Incomappleux Sinixt *nk'mapeleks* thanks for washing out that logging road and protecting the hunting grounds, after the forced evictions, after the burning, the violence, the indifference,

LAKE

UPPER

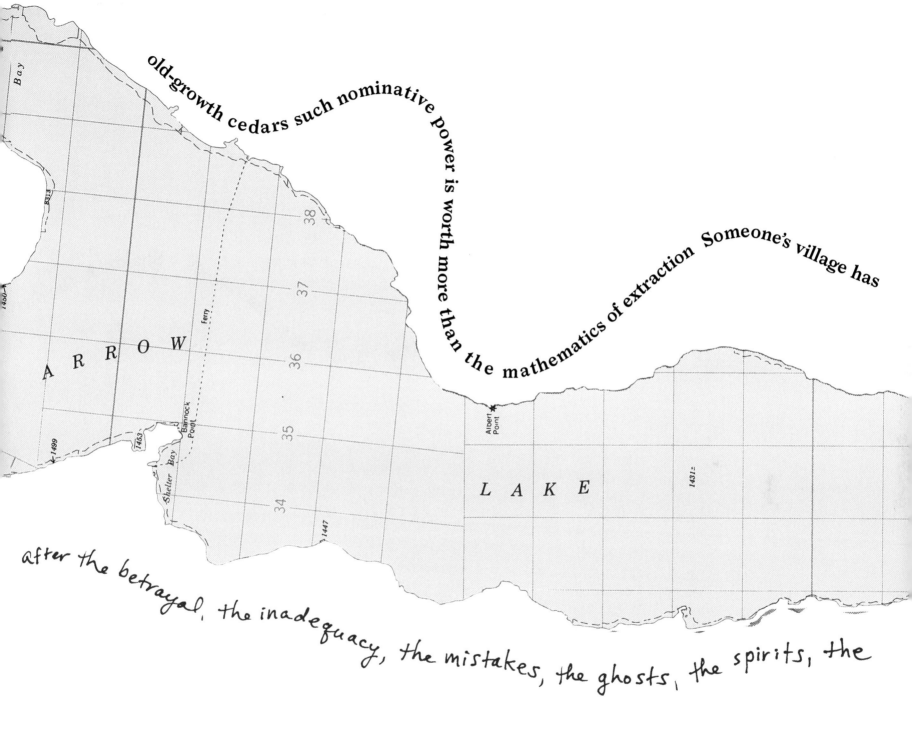

old-growth cedars such nominative power is worth more than the mathematics of extraction   Someone's village has

after the betrayal, the inadequacy, the mistakes, the ghosts, the spirits, the

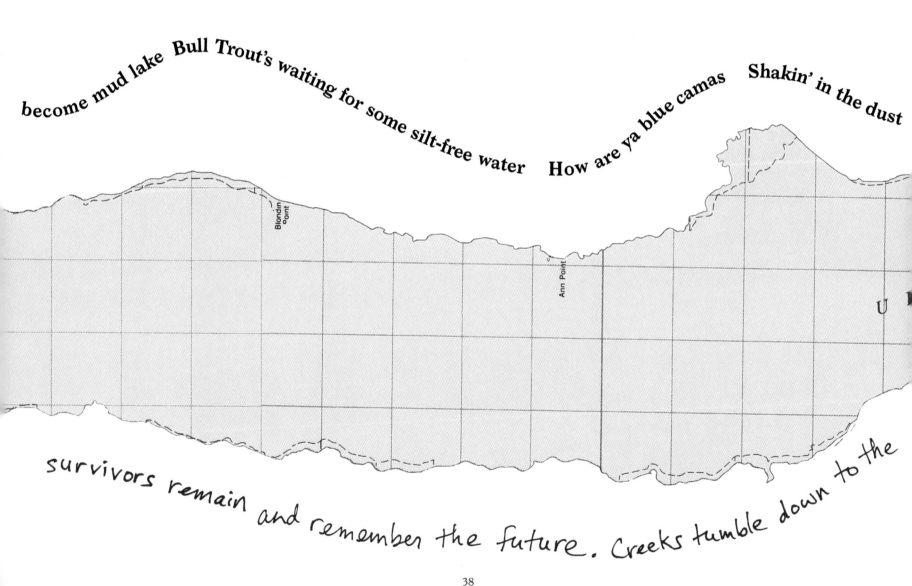

become mud lake Bull Trout's waiting for some silt-free water   How are ya blue camas   Shakin' in the dust

Blondin Point

Ann Point

U

survivors remain and remember the future. Creeks tumble down to the

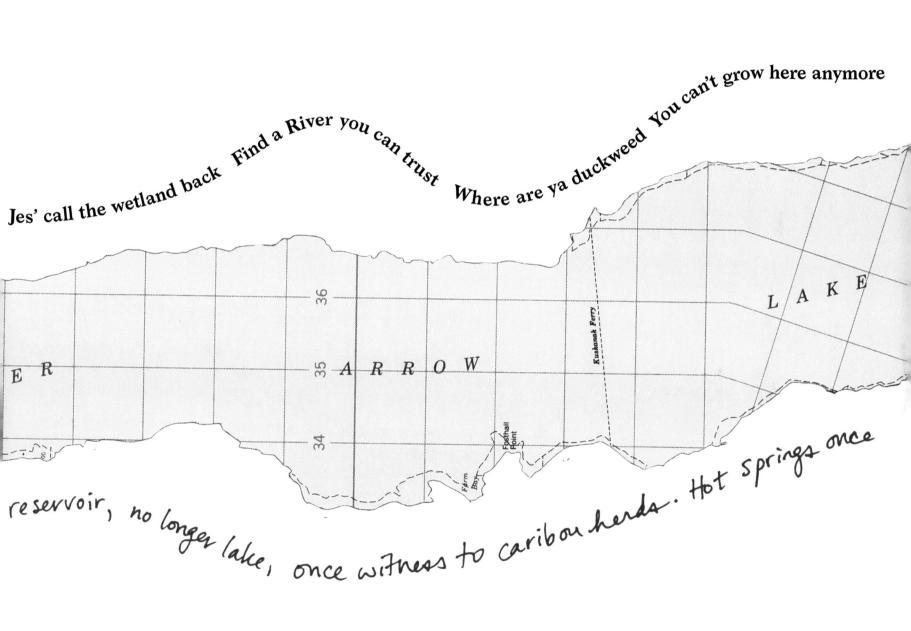

Jes' call the wetland back Find a River you can trust Where are ya duckweed You can't grow here anymore

reservoir, no longer lake, once witness to caribou herds. Hot springs once

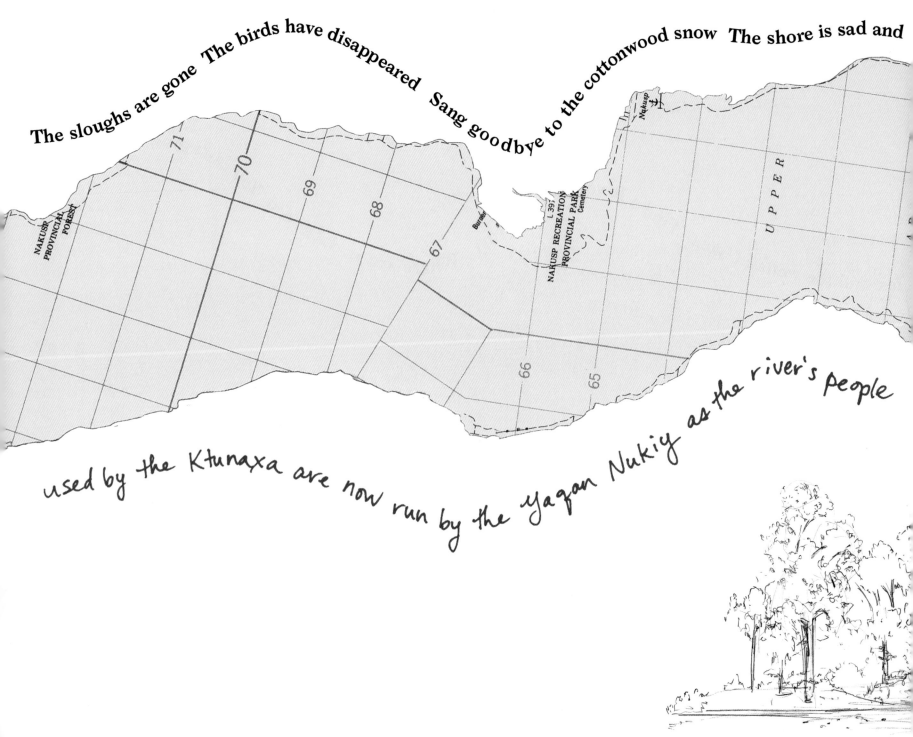

The sloughs are gone The birds have disappeared Sang goodbye to the cottonwood snow The shore is sad and

used by the Ktunaxa are now run by the Yaqan Nukiy as the river's people

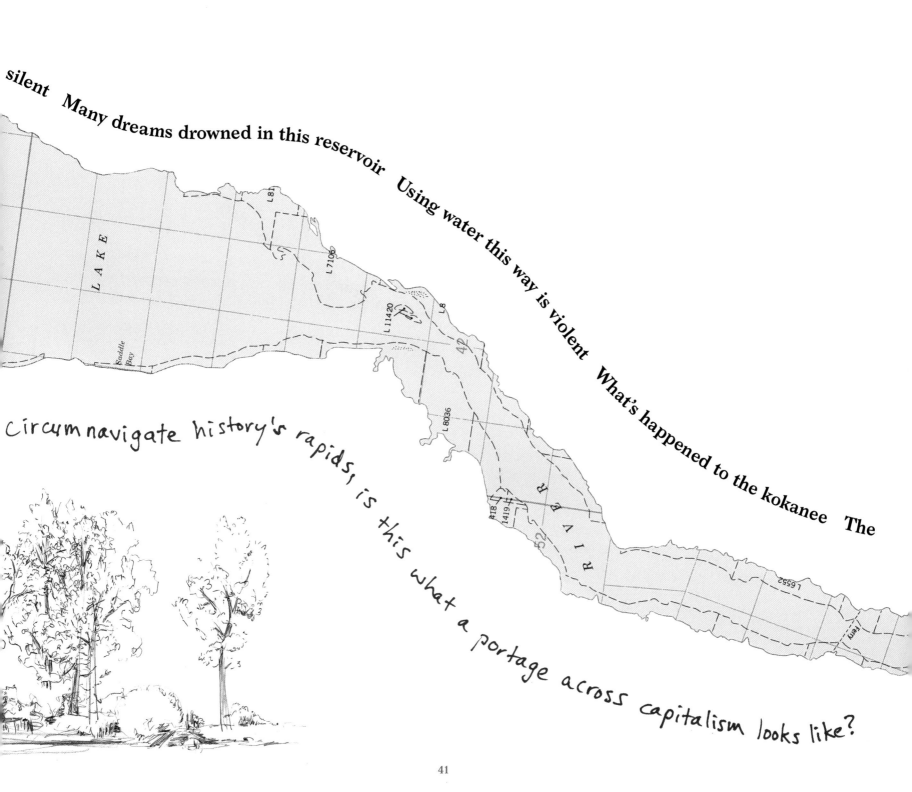

silent   Many dreams drowned in this reservoir   Using water this way is violent   What's happened to the kokanee   The

circumnavigate history's rapids, is this what a portage across capitalism looks like?

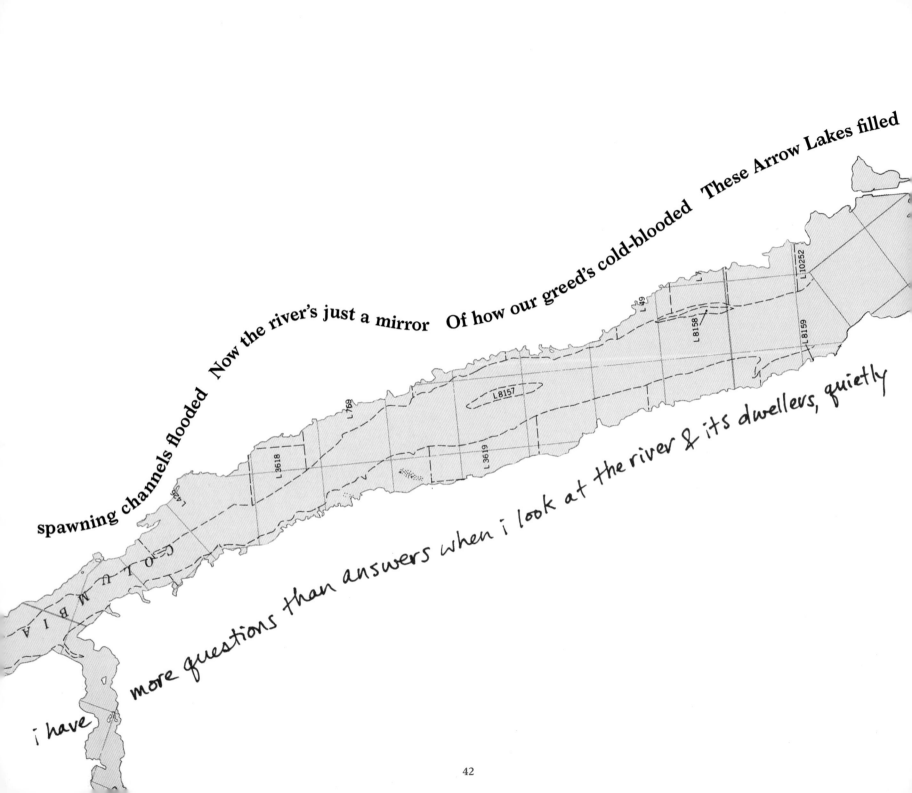

spawning channels flooded Now the river's just a mirror   Of how our greed's cold-blooded   These Arrow Lakes filled

more questions than answers when i look at the river & its dwellers, quietly

i have

42

up and up and killed the estuaries of the creeks flooded fields of grass and drowned the orchards submerged ancestral

stringing a kinship of rivers across its moving parts. from dust to dew, broom bud to butterfly,

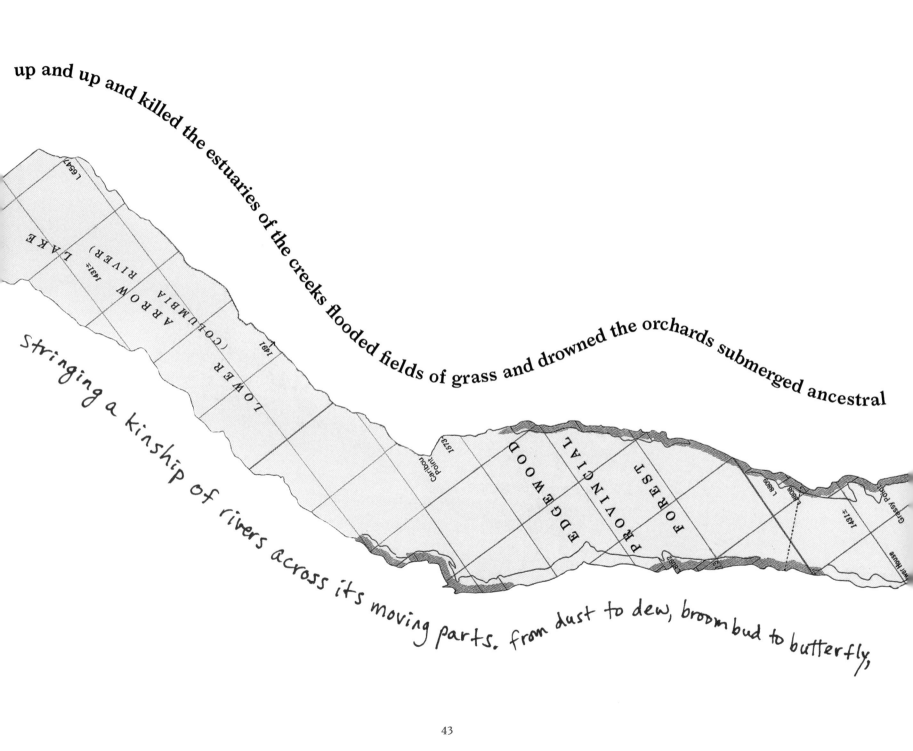

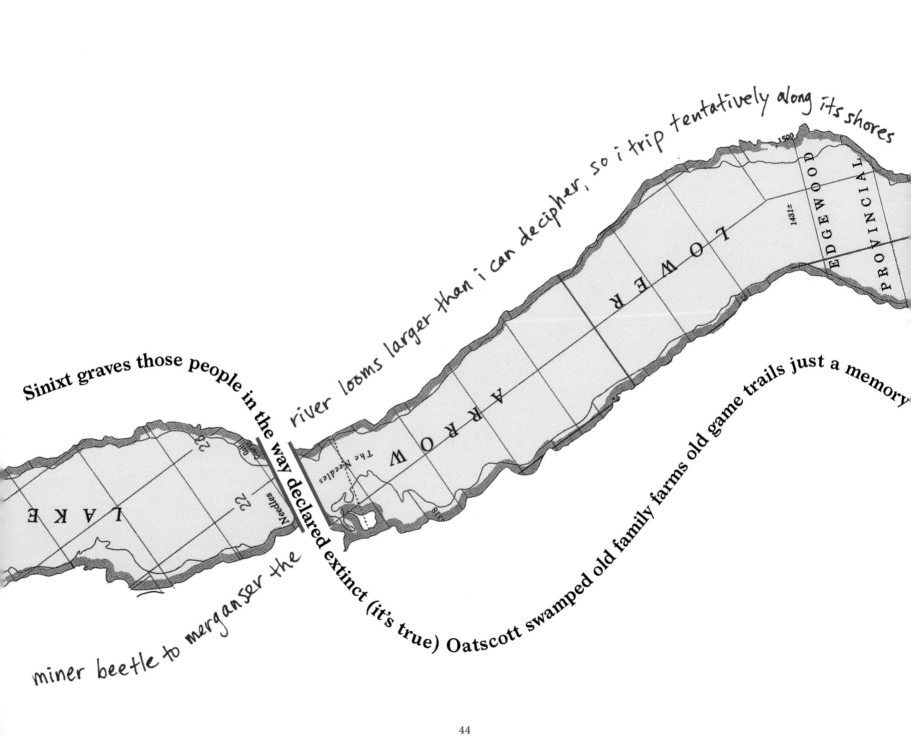

Sinixt graves those people in the way declared extinct (it's true) Oatscott swamped old family farms old game trails just a memory

river looms larger than i can decipher, so i trip tentatively along its shores

miner beetle to merganser the

a grateful guest, witness to ferries gliding over the ruins and ancestors underneath,

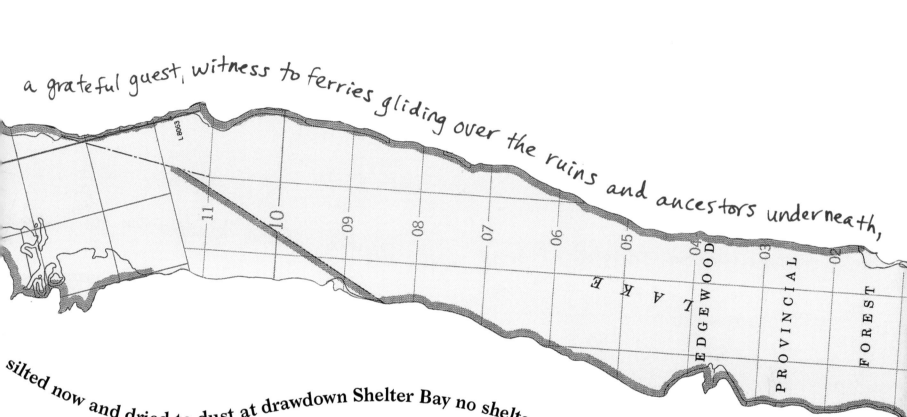

silted now and dried to dust at drawdown Shelter Bay no shelter after all this valley could be filled with love

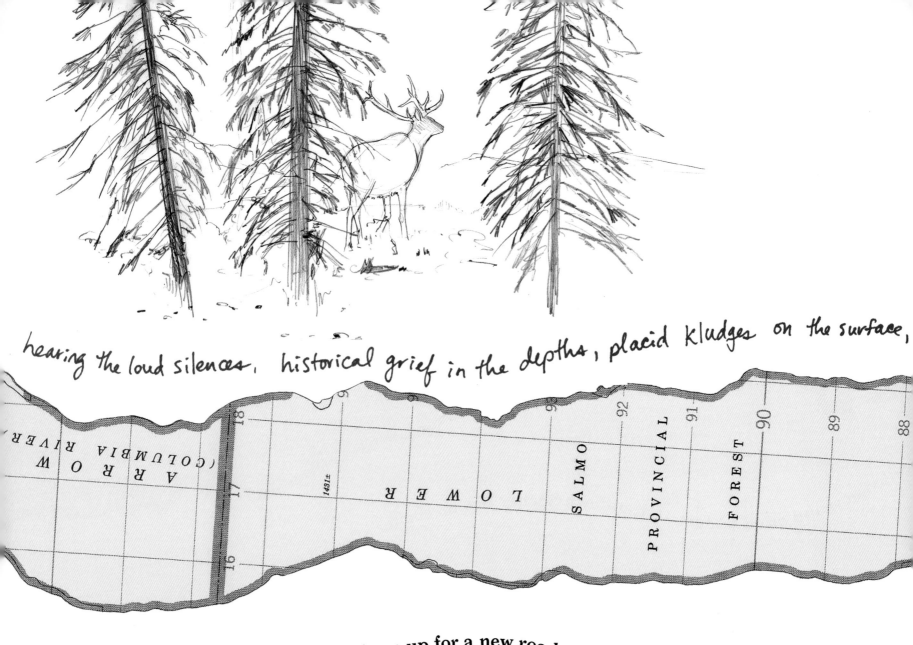

hearing the loud silences, historical grief in the depths, placid Kludges on the surface,

oh lonely animal eyes at Caribou Point blown up for a new road so sing the blues to be this River washed

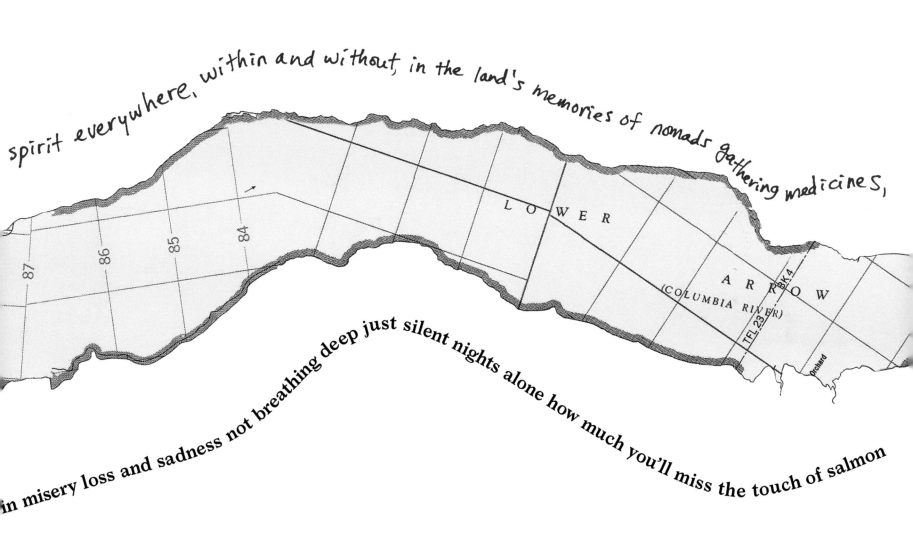

spirit everywhere, within and without, in the land's memories of nomads gathering medicines,

in misery loss and sadness not breathing deep just silent nights alone how much you'll miss the touch of salmon

children picking huckleberries, autonomous communities in balance with what a solar budget provides,

redd and sedge grass edge the churning of the Minto up to Arrowhead (and then the burning too) yeh! ain't

LAKE

29 30 L O W E R

A R R O W

Shields
Point

Will the salmon ever

life's brilliance before the artificial stop, the stagnation, the invasion. yet return

LAKE

Marina

Yacht Club

Driftwood Beach

Keenle Dam

this dam messed up your plan to keep this spirit flowing with respect Will the riparian ever be repaired?

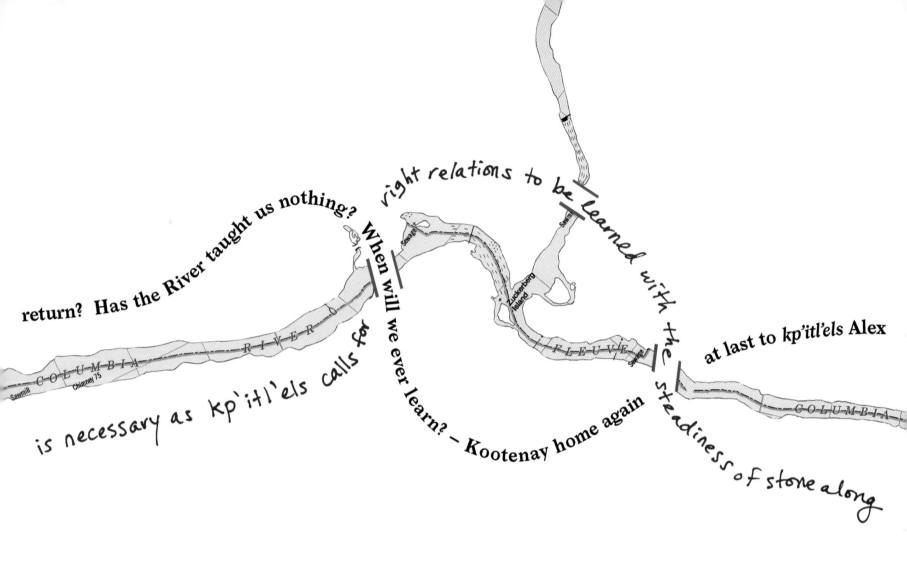

return? Has the River taught us nothing? right relations to be learned with the **When will we ever learn? – Kootenay home again** at last to kp'itl'els Alex is necessary as kp'itl'els calls for steadiness of stone along

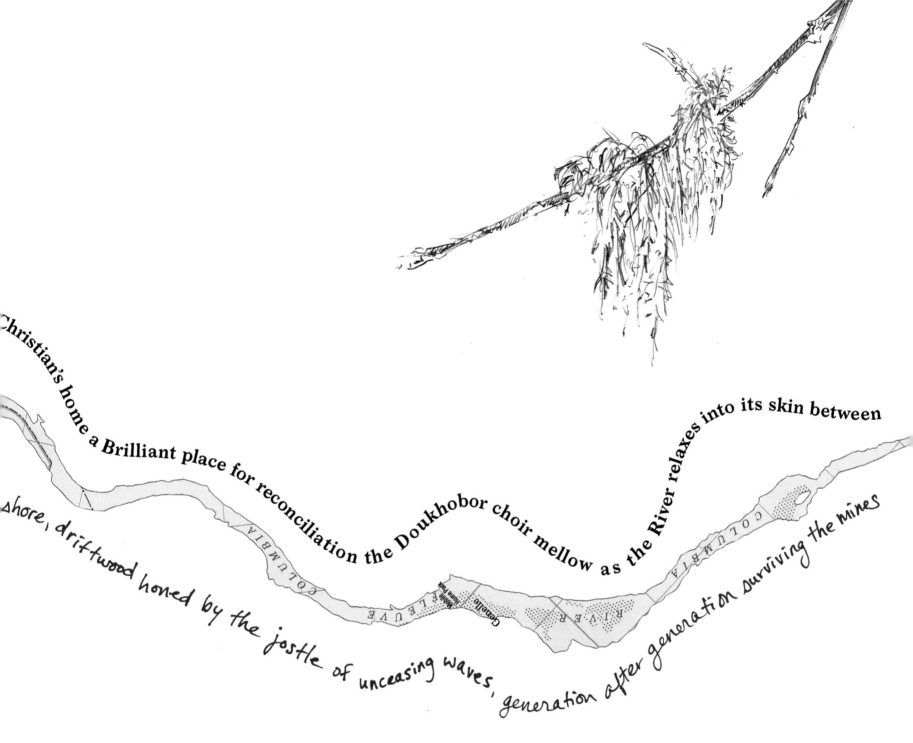

Christian's home a Brilliant place for reconciliation the Doukhobor choir mellow as the River relaxes into its skin between shore, driftwood honed by the jostle of unceasing waves, generation after generation surviving the mines

COLUMBIA FLEUVE Mobile Home Park Genelle COLUMBIA RIVER COLUMBIA

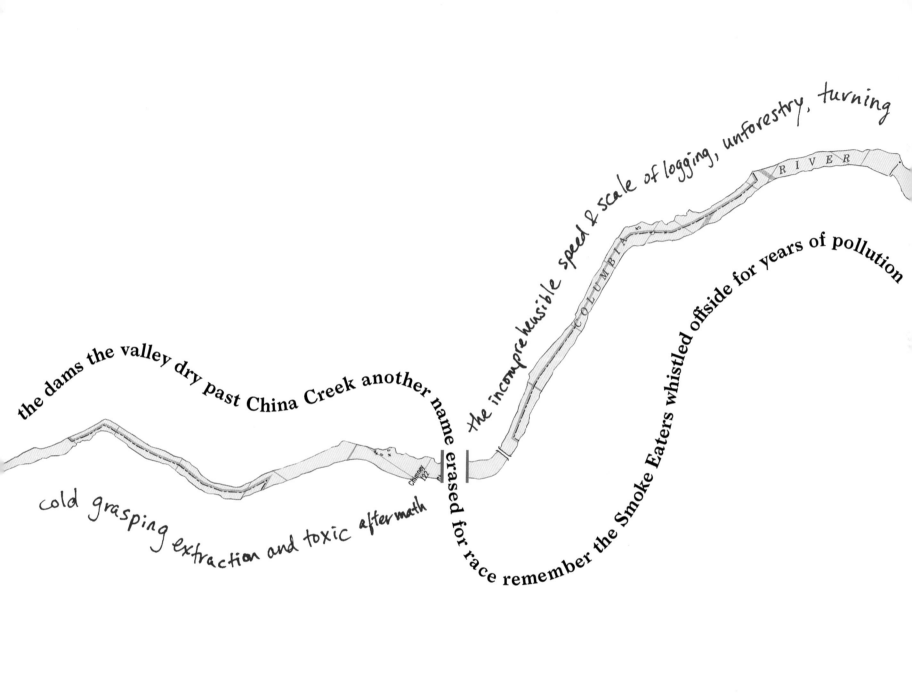

the dams the valley dry past China Creek another name erased for race remember the Smoke Eaters whistled offside for years of pollution

the incomprehensible speed & scale of logging, unforestry, turning

cold grasping extraction and toxic aftermath

RIVER

COLUMBIA

Chimney 192

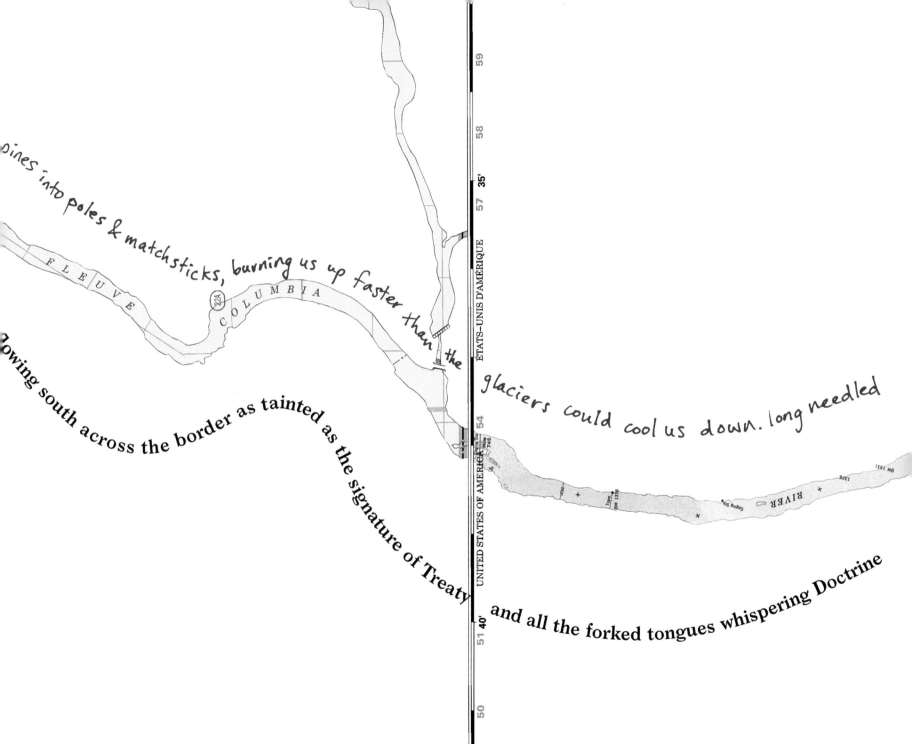

pines into poles & matchsticks, burning us up faster than the

glaciers could cool us down. long needled

owing south across the border as tainted as the signature of Treaty

and all the forked tongues whispering Doctrine

FLEUVE

COLUMBIA

22A

ÉTATS–UNIS D'AMÉRIQUE

UNITED STATES OF AMERICA

RIVER

59

58

57 35'

54

51 40'

50

49

53

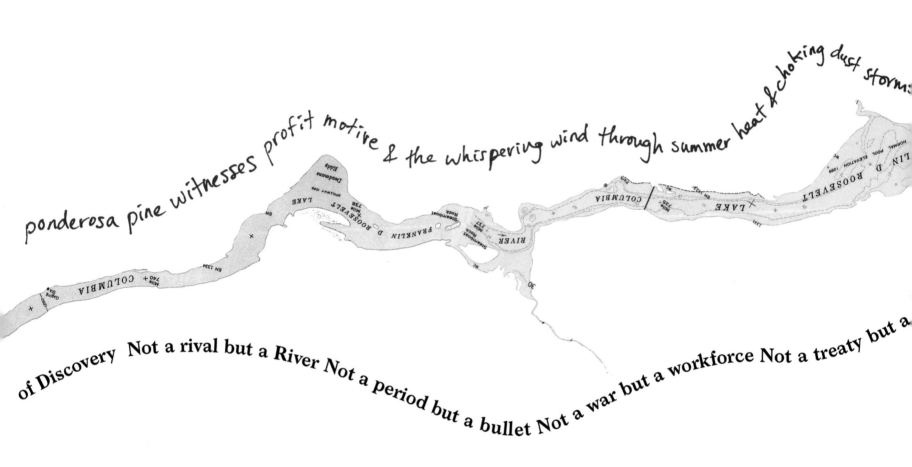

ponderosa pine witnesses profit motive & the whispering wind through summer heat & choking dust storms

of Discovery Not a rival but a River Not a period but a bullet Not a war but a workforce Not a treaty but a

through dolled up American imperialism that turns freedom into reservations imposes imaginary but policed

...rait d'union Not the floods of '48 but Be Prepared Not the International Joint Commission but the Army Corps

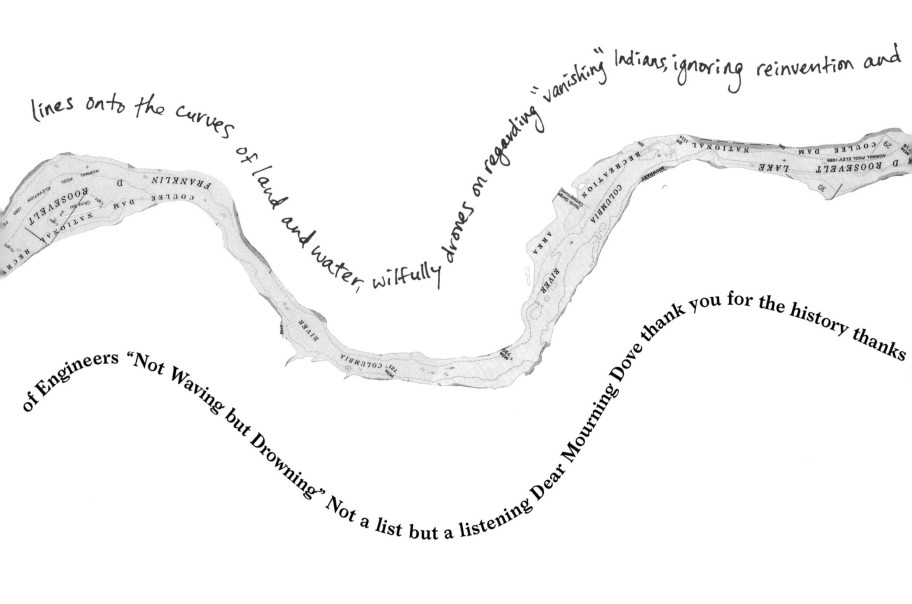

lines onto the curves of land and water, wilfully drones on regarding "vanishing" Indians, ignoring reinvention and

of Engineers "Not Waving but Drowning" Not a list but a listening Dear Mourning Dove thank you for the history thanks

persistance in the face of attempted genocide, forced removal, starvation & military brutality. Imperial delirium

for sharing your Salishan story while standing in the doorway not doing any harm you show this River as a map of white and black No Trespass

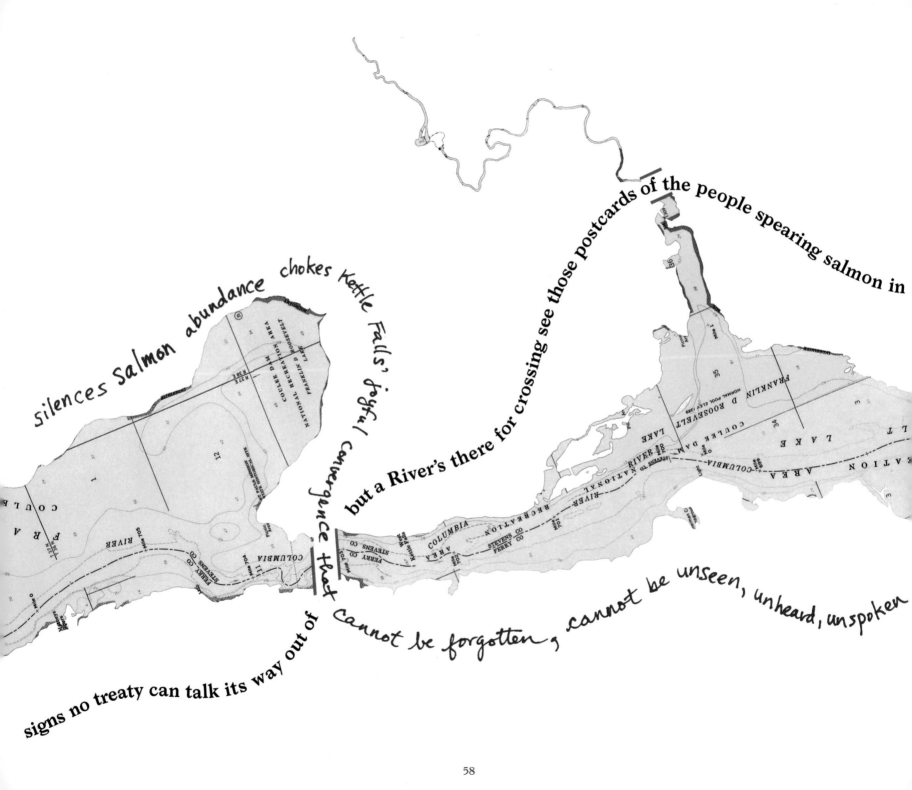

silences Salmon abundance chokes Kettle Falls' joyful convergence that

but a River's there for crossing see those postcards of the people spearing salmon in

cannot be forgotten, cannot be unseen, unheard, unspoken

signs no treaty can talk its way out of

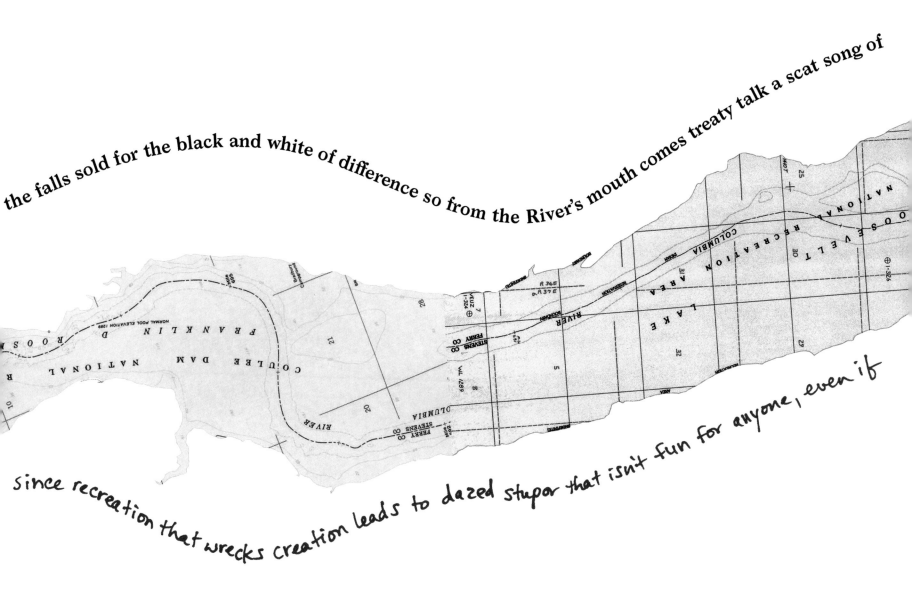

the falls sold for the black and white of difference so from the River's mouth comes treaty talk a scat song of

since recreation that wrecks creation leads to dazed stupor that isn't fun for anyone, even if

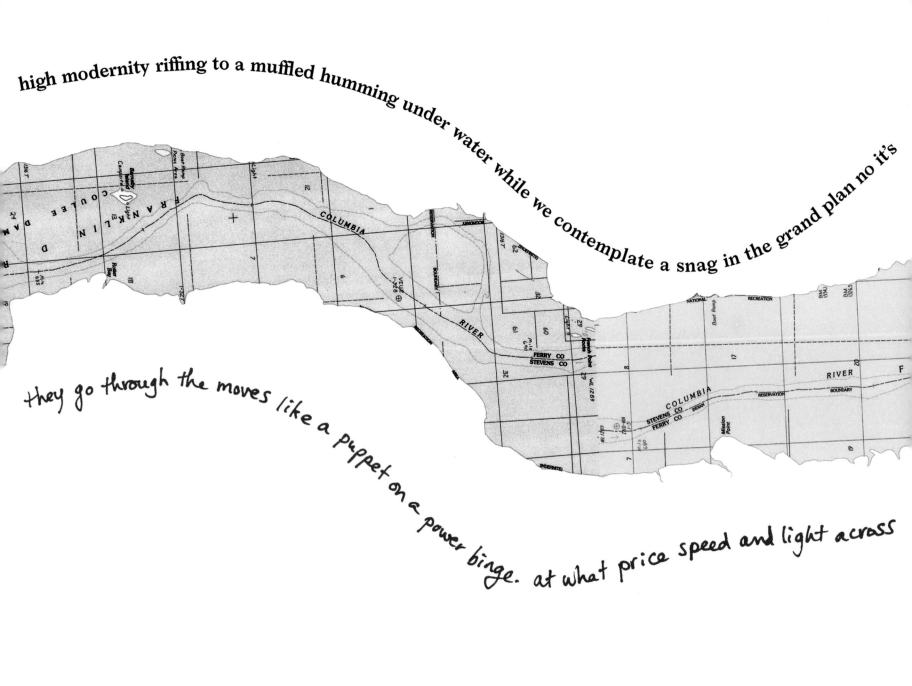

high modernity riffing to a muffled humming under water while we contemplate a snag in the grand plan no it's

they go through the moves like a puppet on a power binge. at what price speed and light across

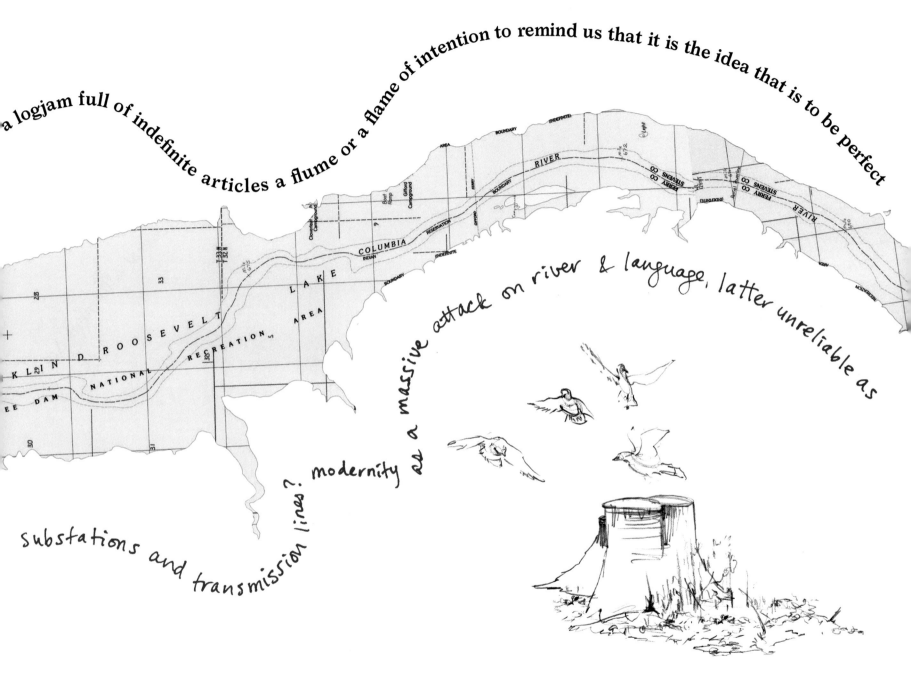

a logjam full of indefinite articles a flume or a flame of intention to remind us that it is the idea that is to be perfect

a massive attack on river & language, latter unreliable as

modernity as

substations and transmission lines?

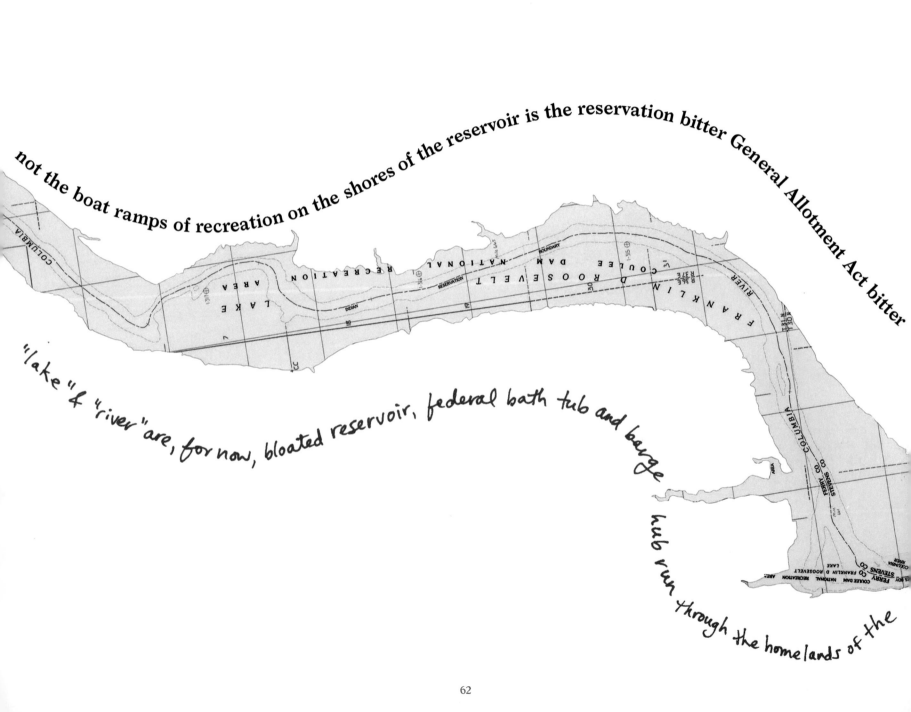

not the boat ramps of recreation on the shores of the reservoir is the reservation bitter General Allotment Act bitter

"lake" & "river" are, for now, bloated reservoir, federal bath tub and barge hub run through the homelands of the

Executive Order Turtle Island bitten by its own rapids north of O-Ra-Pak-En Creek trickling into Franklin Coulee's

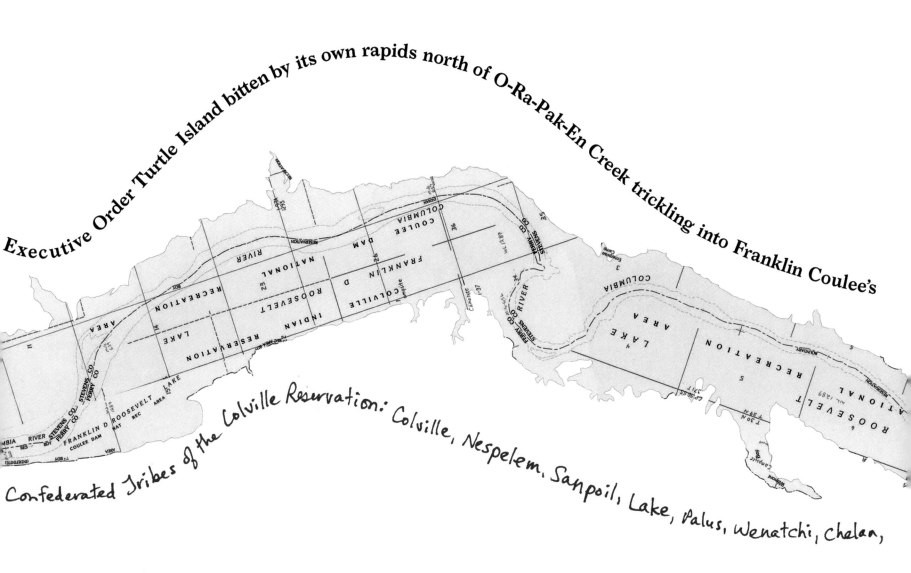

Confederated Tribes of the Colville Reservation: Colville, Nespelem, Sanpoil, Lake, Palus, Wenatchi, Chelan,

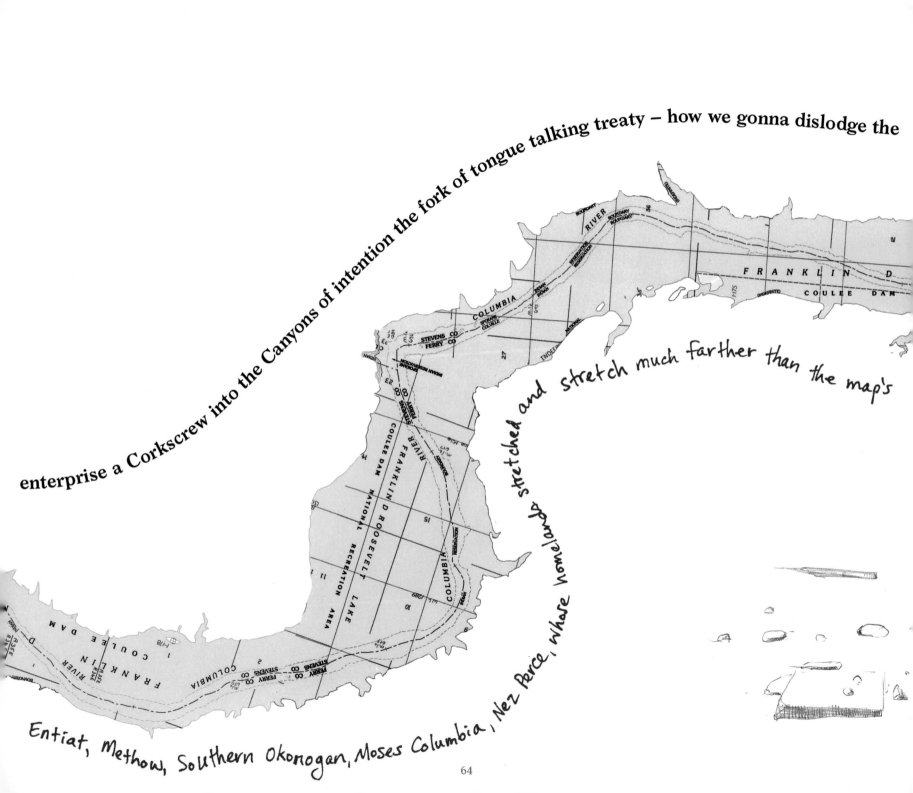

enterprise a Corkscrew into the Canyons of intention the fork of tongue talking treaty – how we gonna dislodge the

and stretch much farther than the map's

where homelands stretched

Entiat, Methow, Southern Okonogan, Moses Columbia, Nez Perce,

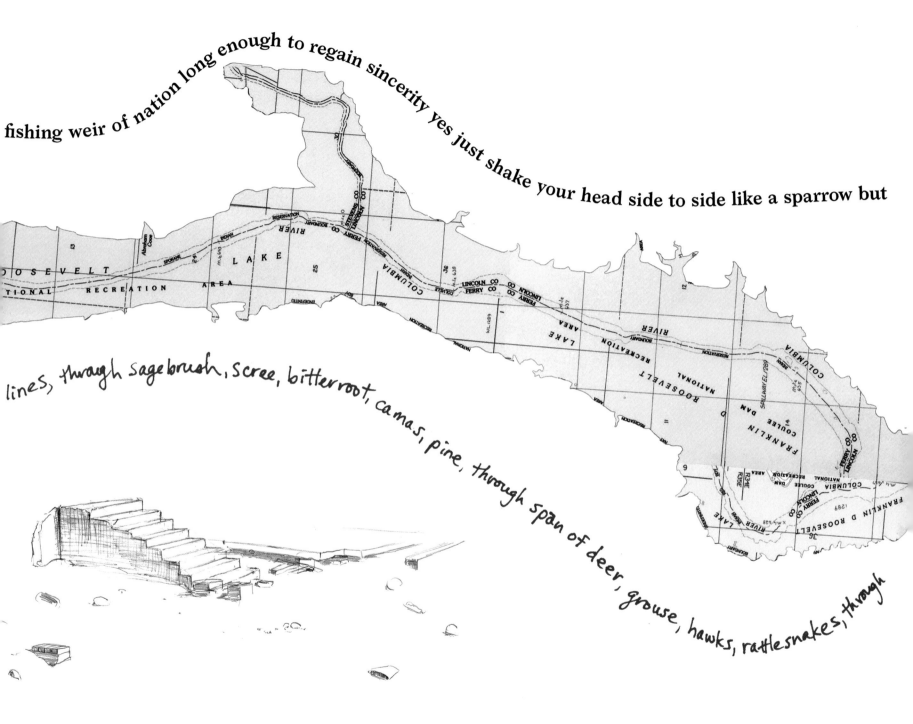

fishing weir of nation long enough to regain sincerity yes just shake your head side to side like a sparrow but

lines, through sagebrush, scree, bitterroot, camas, pine, through span of deer, grouse, hawks, rattlesnakes, through

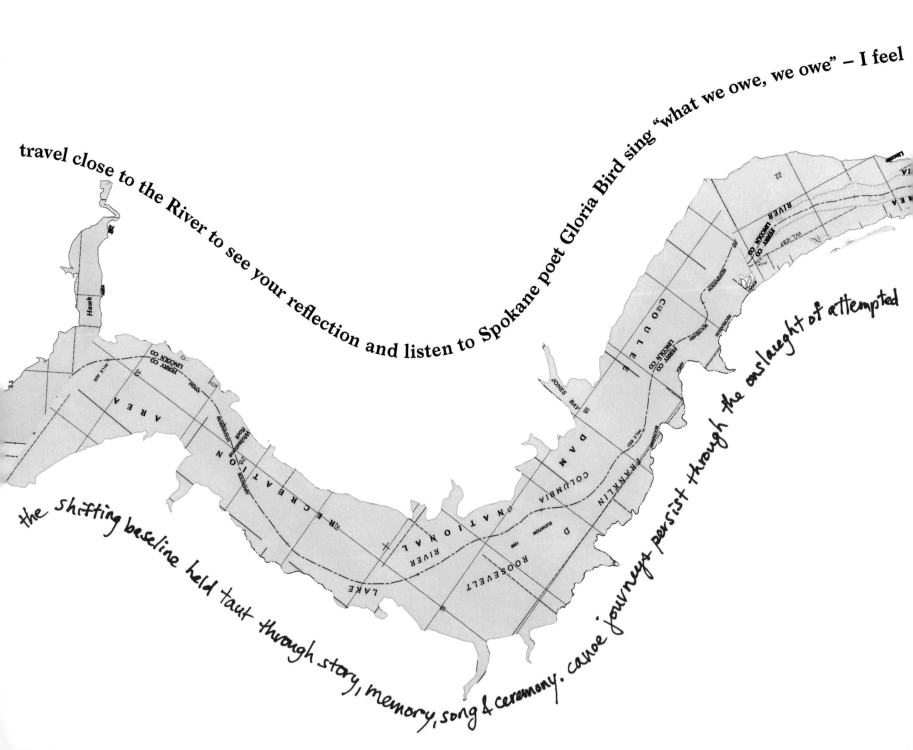

travel close to the River to see your reflection and listen to Spokane poet Gloria Bird sing "what we owe, we owe" – I feel

the shifting baseline held taut through story, memory, song & ceremony. canoe journeys persist through the onslaught of attempted

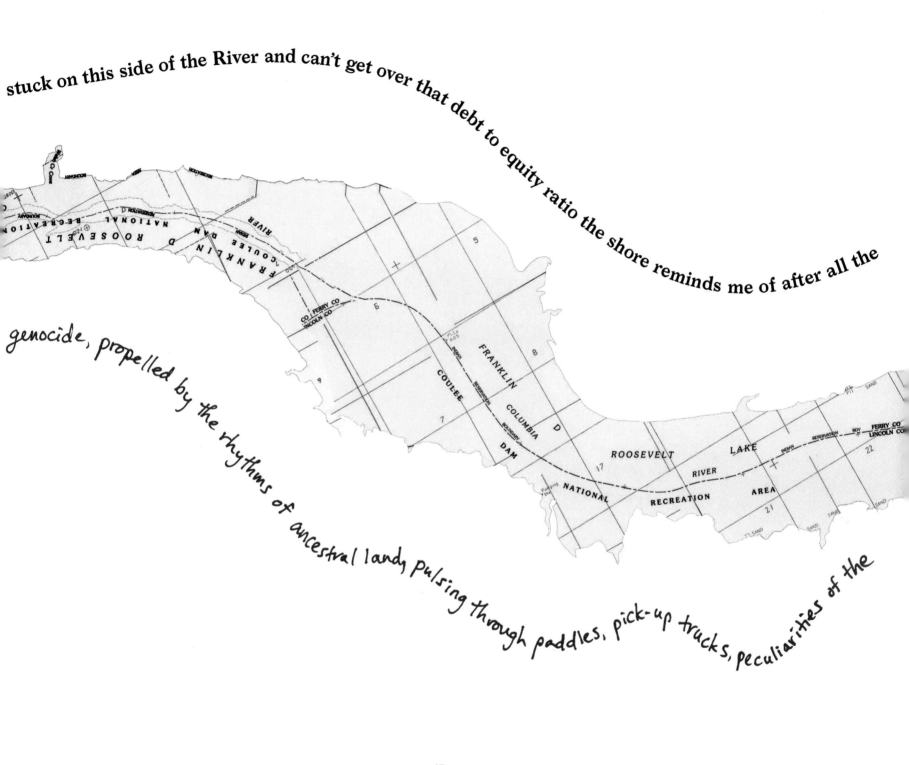

stuck on this side of the River and can't get over that debt to equity ratio the shore reminds me of after all the

genocide, propelled by the rhythms of ancestral lands, pulsing through paddles, pick-up trucks, peculiarities of the

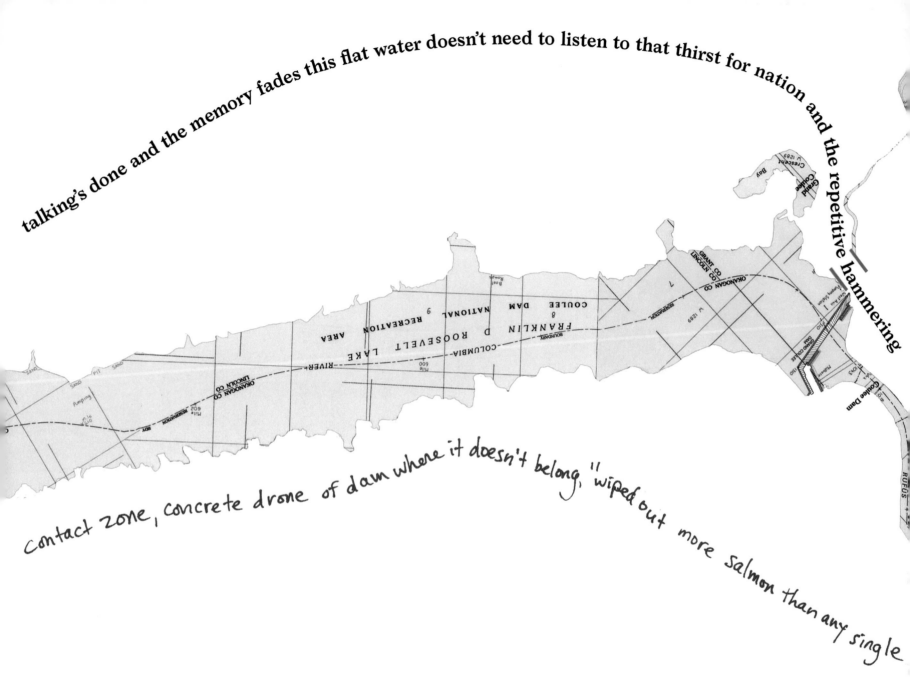

talking's done and the memory fades this flat water doesn't need to listen to that thirst for nation and the repetitive hammering

contact zone, concrete drone of dam where it doesn't belong, "wiped out more salmon than any single of the Grand Plan's gavel or the thud of ambivalence that irrigates my ears as if a lake would rather be a city don't let the names

structure in American history," concomitant manufacturer of depression, alcoholism, starvation, hidden hunger,

replace the reflection of intention could it really be as simple as out under the apple tree then don't stand on

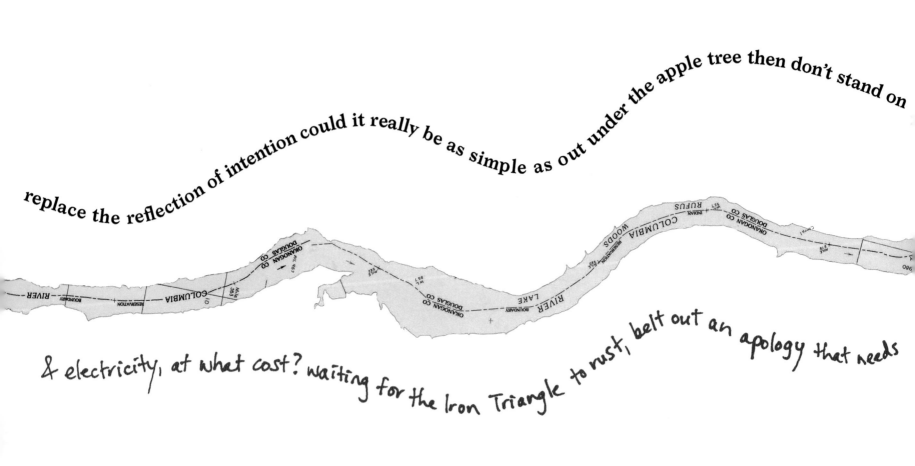

& electricity, at what cost? waiting for the Iron Triangle to rust, belt out an apology that needs

ceremony or bite your tongue but remember to return those salmon bones to the water turning truth into a verb —

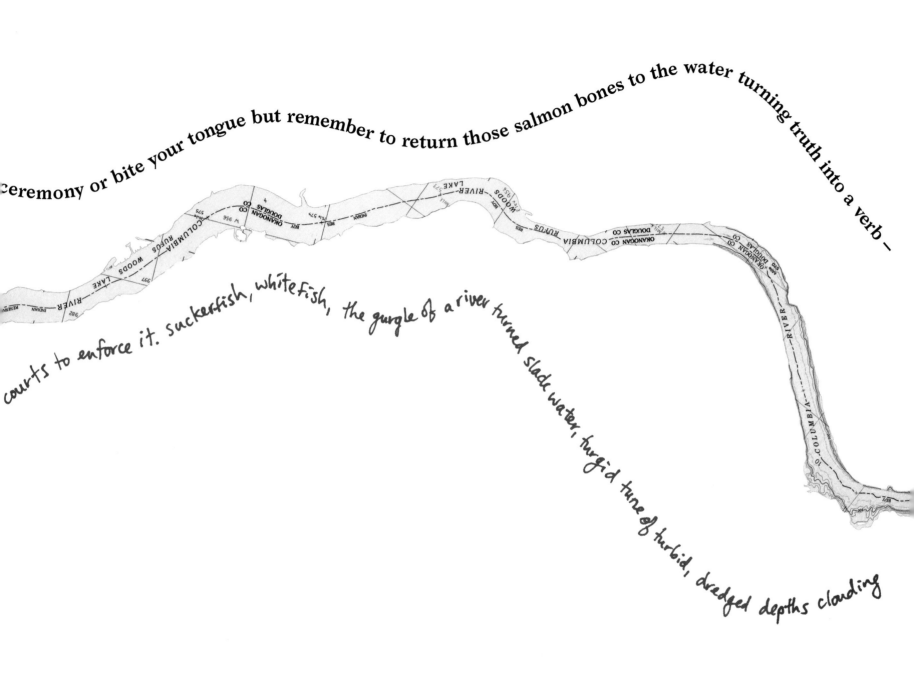

courts to enforce it. Suckerfish, whitefish, the gurgle of a river turned slack water, turgid tune of turbid, dredged depths clouding

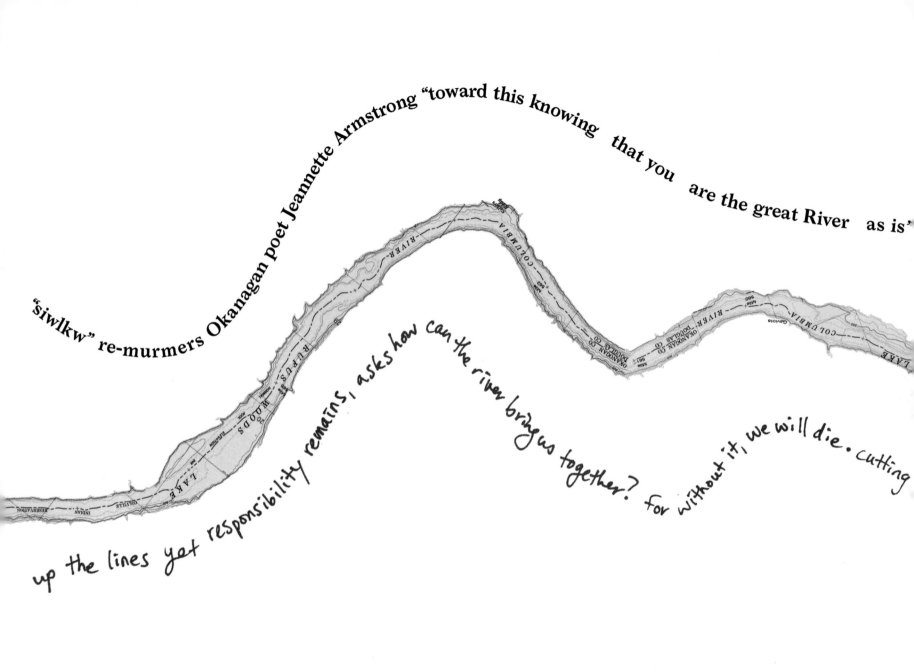

"siwlkw" re-murmers Okanagan poet Jeannette Armstrong "toward this knowing that you are the great River as is'

up the lines yet responsibility remains, asks how can the river brings us together? for without it, we will die. cutting

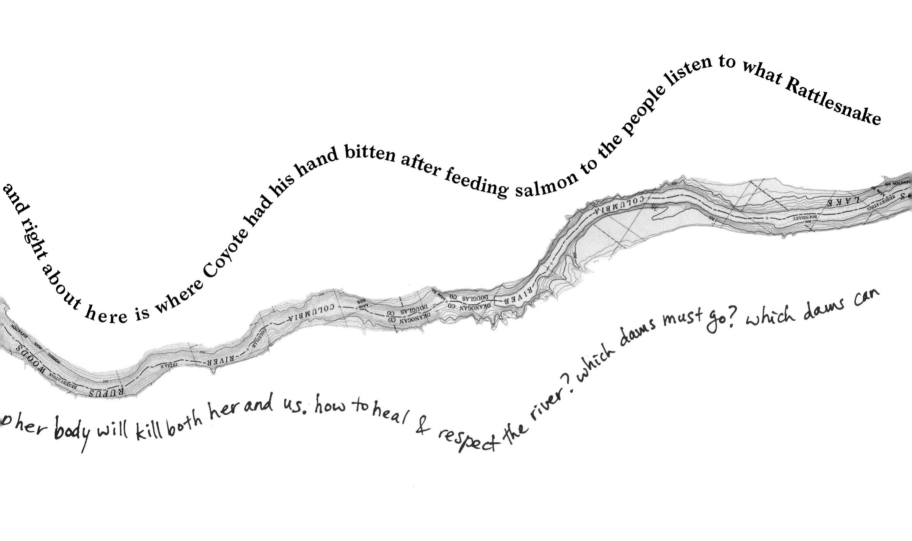

and right about here is where Coyote had his hand bitten after feeding salmon to the people listen to what Rattlesnake

o her body will kill both her and us. how to heal & respect the river? which dams must go? which dams can

learned about thirst from the River – stand still in the clarity of this quiet still water silt toes pointed downriver

stay? Without maintenance, things fall apart. And so it bears repeating the tribal nations of this watershed: Kalispel, Kootenai, Salish, Flathead, Coeur d'Alene

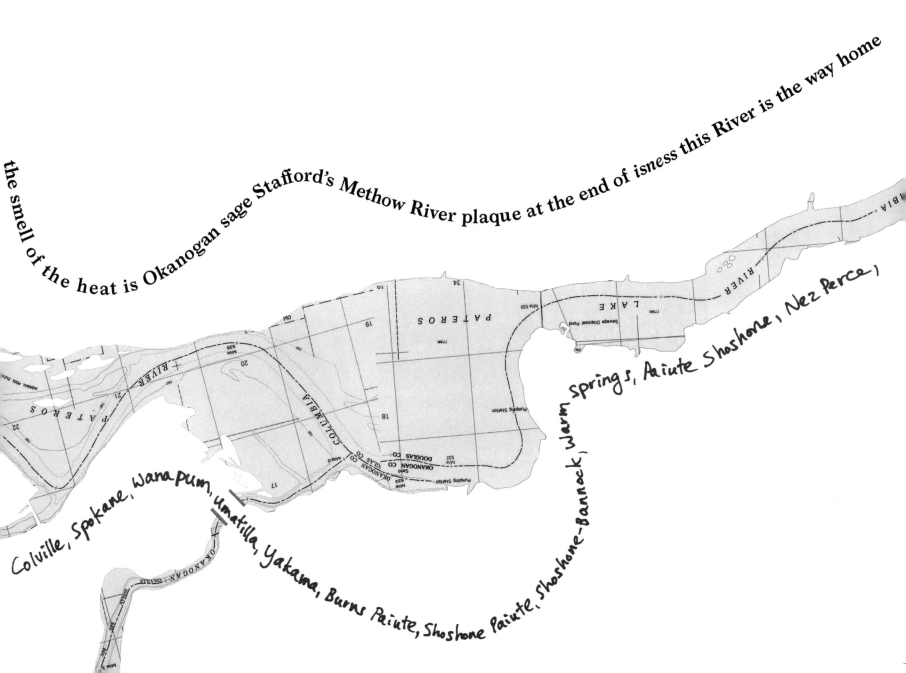

the smell of the heat is Okanogan sage Stafford's Methow River plaque at the end of isness this River is the way home

Colville, Spokane, Wanapum, Umatilla, Yakama, Burns Paiute, Shoshone Paiute, Shoshone-Bannock, Warm Springs, Paiute Shoshone, Nez Perce,

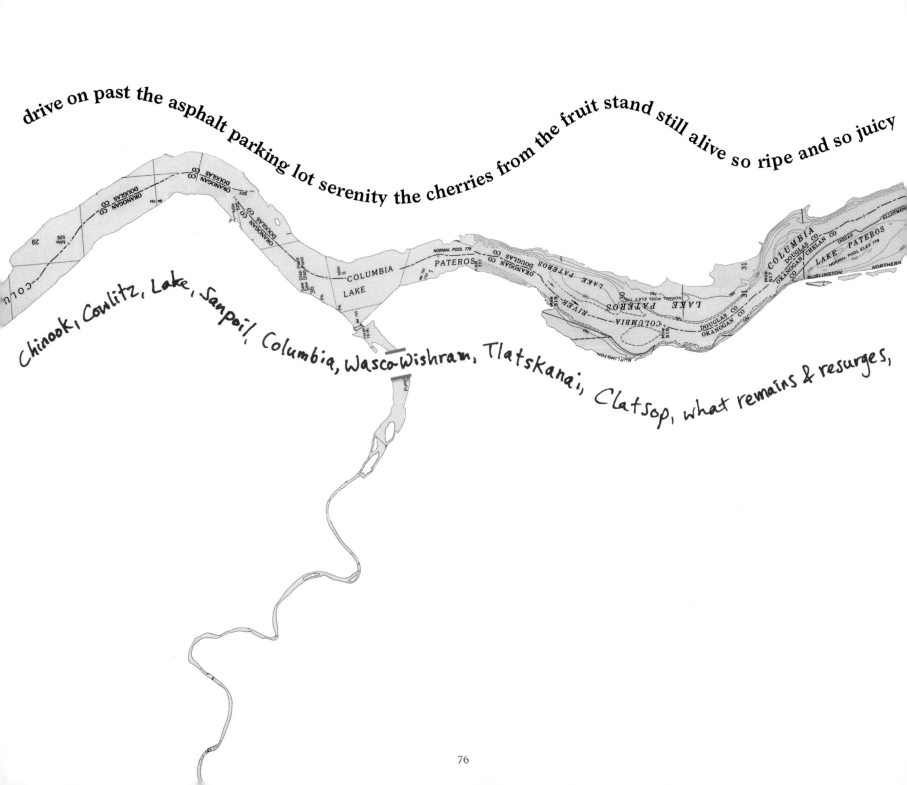

drive on past the asphalt parking lot serenity the cherries from the fruit stand still alive so ripe and so juicy

Chinook, Cowlitz, Lake, Sanpoil, Columbia, Wasco-Wishram, Tlatskanai, Clatsop, what remains & resurges, try to hear what the River says as we spit the pits into the irrigated grass the air heavy and mesmerized as the sprinklers

wave by wave, generation by generation as blood memory, cell memory, is river memory, remembering the future for the

click under a cloud of insecticide sprayed over the orchards while the River hums the livin' is easy they could

ENTI LAKE ENTIAT NORMAL POOL ELEVATION 707 RIVER RIVER COLUMBIA GREAT NORTHERN COLUMBIA CHELAN CO DOUGLAS CO COLUMBIA RIVER ENTIAT

ones yet to come, who matter even if we do not know their names, who remain relatives to salmon,

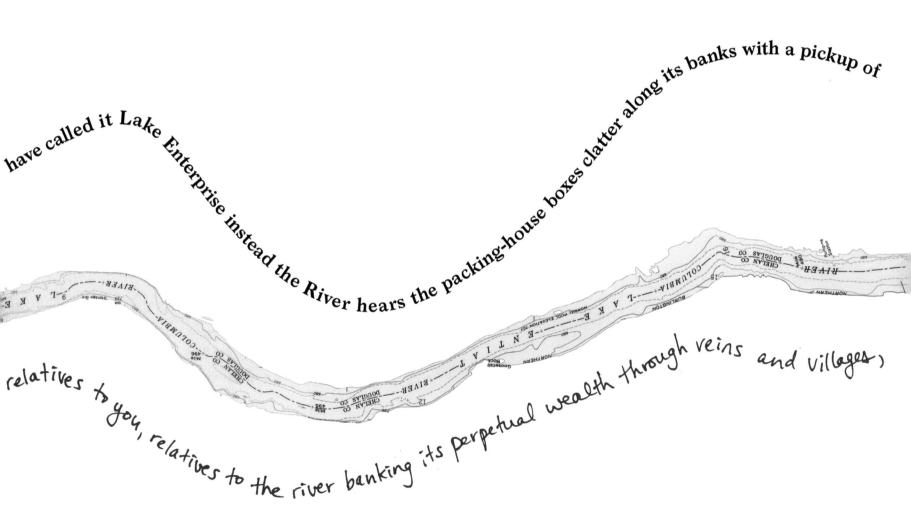

have called it Lake Enterprise instead the River hears the packing-house boxes clatter along its banks with a pickup of

relatives to you, relatives to the river banking its perpetual wealth through veins and villages,

pickers on a dusty side road – it's what we hear and usually what we say but nadie me comprende the River's

trees and terrain, song and starlight. farmworkers know the vast apple orchards in Spanish, working the

voice is the sound our body makes when we're sleepwalking through the abyss of our own presence in the world

temporarily green monocultural agribusinesses shift by precarious shift, but apples are no substitute

– flesh against bone water over bedrock even if the rapids are gone this water's the story we must tell ourselves we have to think

for the salmon abundance at Kettle Falls, now

silenced by Grand Coulee, traumatic returns repeat

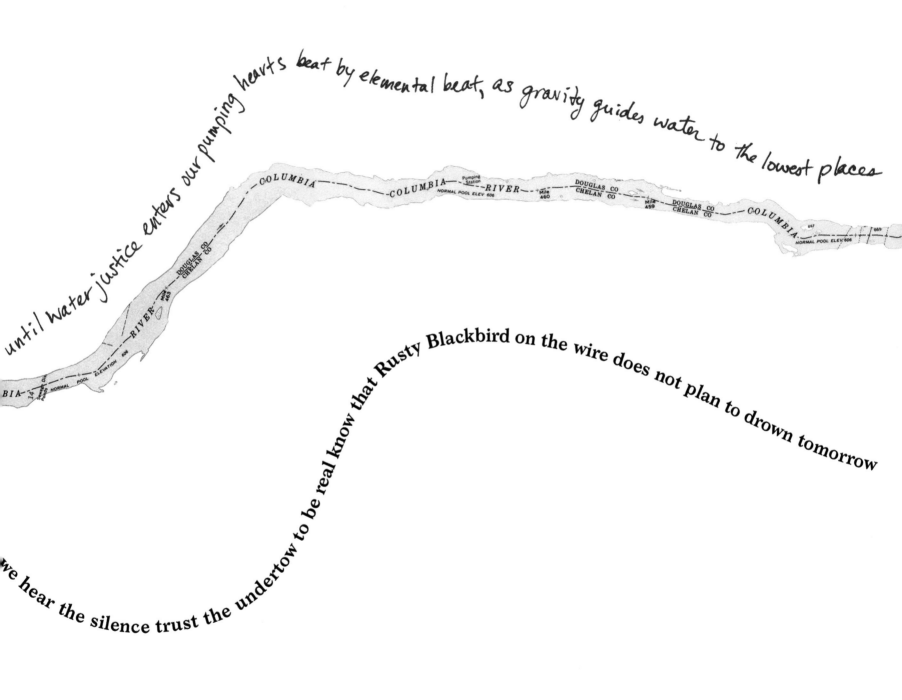

until water justice enters our pumping hearts beat by elemental beat, as gravity guides water to the lowest places

we hear the silence trust the undertow to be real know that Rusty Blackbird on the wire does not plan to drown tomorrow

83

the necessary ones who were here before the dams & who will be here after the dams turn into rubble

despite our grand plans and irrelevant expectations the River invents itself a mighty fine current of thought

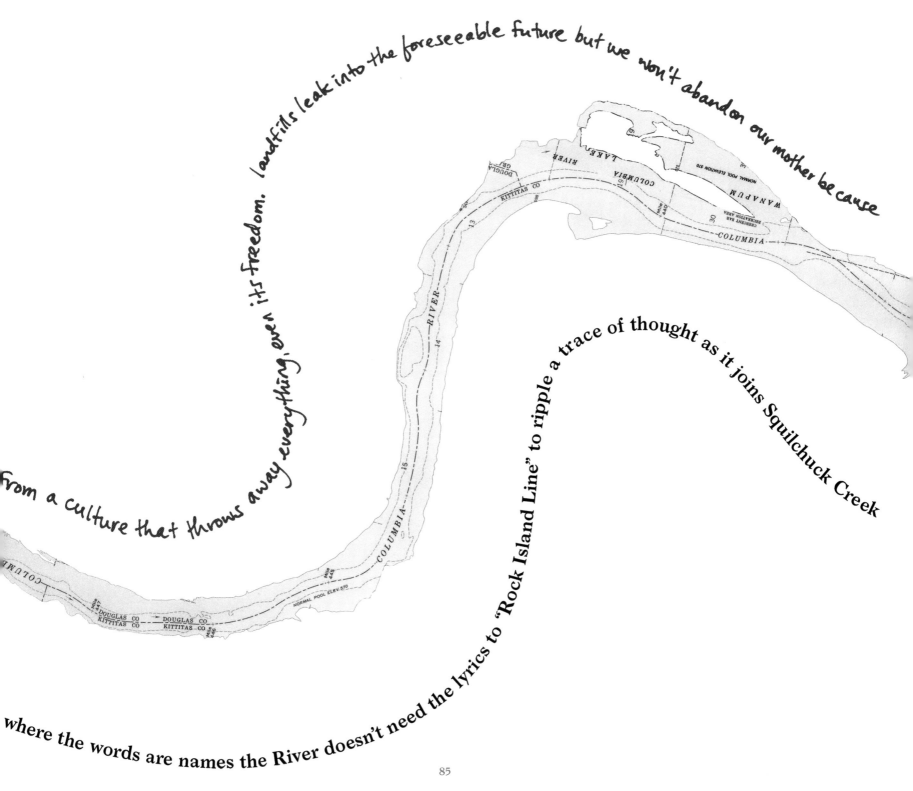

landfills leak into the foreseeable future but we won't abandon our mother because

from a culture that throws away everything, even its freedom.

as it joins Squilchuck Creek

to ripple a trace of thought

where the words are names the River doesn't need the lyrics to "Rock Island Line"

she is poisoned. we learn from the Wanapum, surrounded by nuclear waste, the army's firing range, corporate

to nibble at the basalt doesn't stop to think couldn't wait to get to Voltage to resist the analogy that you can

orchards & the dam, yet still renewing their relationship with the land, still river guardians,

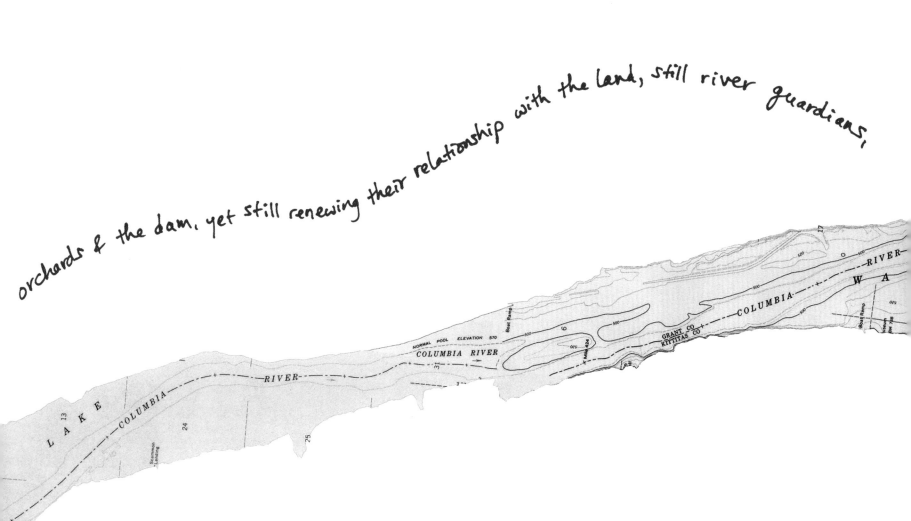

learn to swim by climbing a ladder the pressure to stay afloat or drop like a stone is this the work of

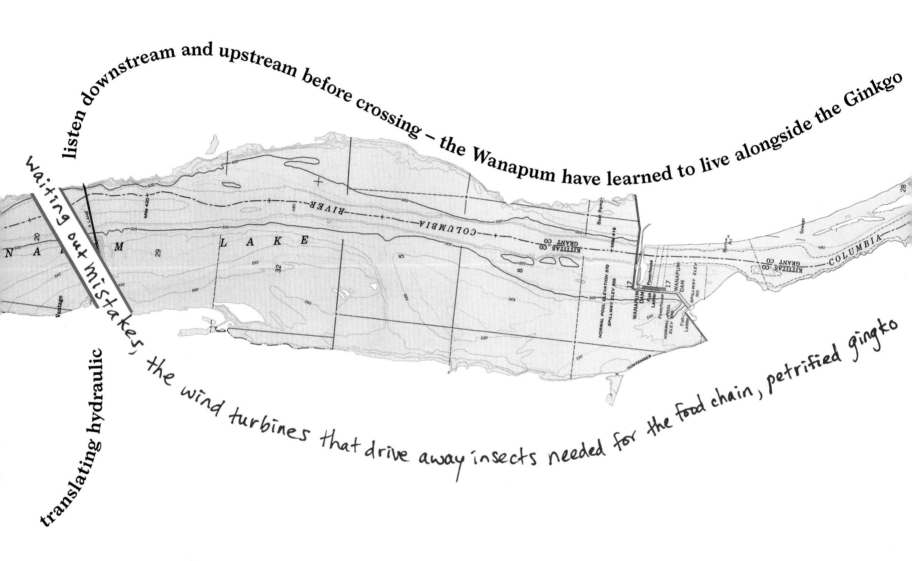

listen downstream and upstream before crossing – the Wanapum have learned to live alongside the Ginkgo

waiting out mistakes, the wind turbines that drive away insects needed for the food chain, petrified gingko

translating hydraulic

and put up with the white man's spelling mistakes the advantage being they know this River will still be here long

Witnessing the static of transmission lines, medicine in the midst of disaster, the Wanapum awaken land ethics

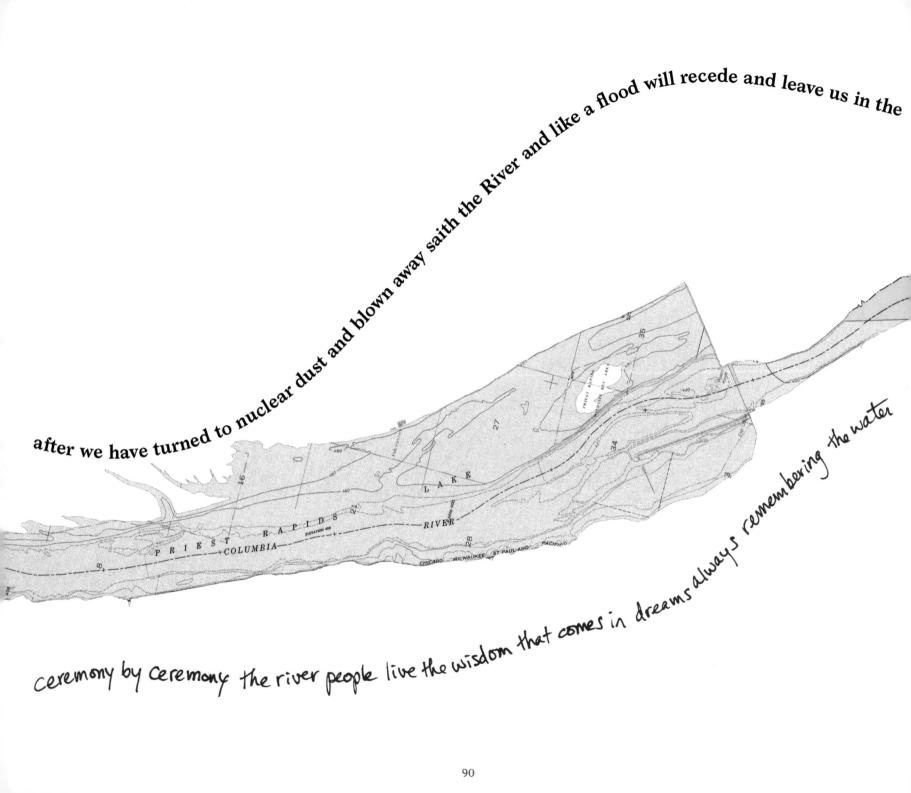

after we have turned to nuclear dust and blown away saith the River and like a flood will recede and leave us in the

ceremony by ceremony the river people live the wisdom that comes in dreams always remembering the water

reach clutching at straws or at least the grape vines along the Wahluke Slope interpellating my name to listen

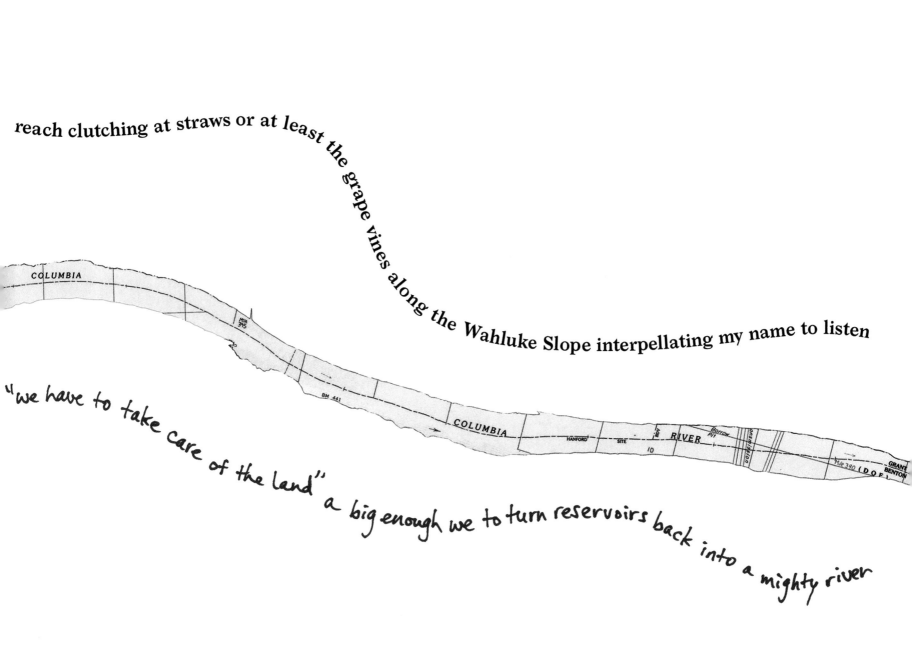

COLUMBIA

BM 441

COLUMBIA RIVER

HANFORD SITE

GRANT BENTON

"we have to take care of the land" a big enough we to turn reservoirs back into a mighty river

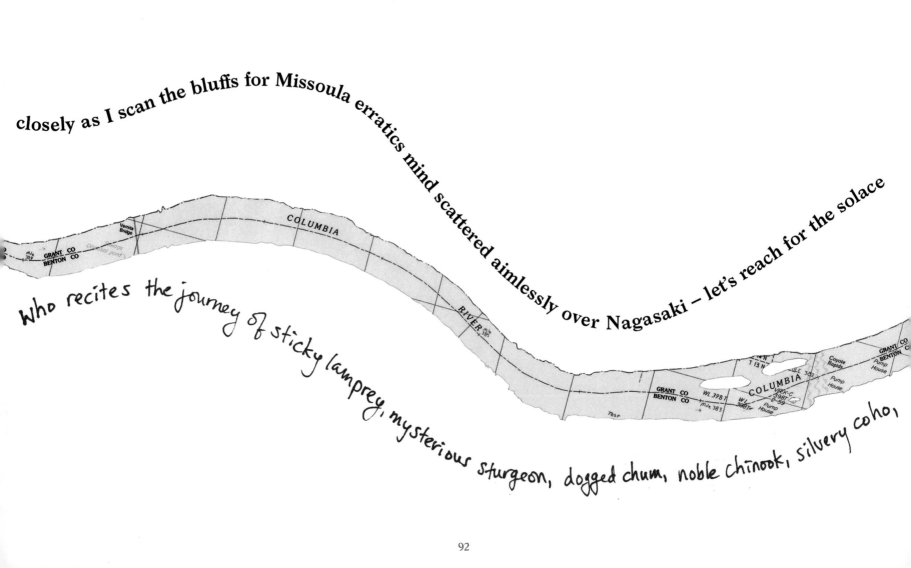

closely as I scan the bluffs for Missoula erratics mind scattered aimlessly over Nagasaki – let's reach for the solace

Who recites the journey of sticky lamprey, mysterious sturgeon, dogged chum, noble chinook, silvery coho,

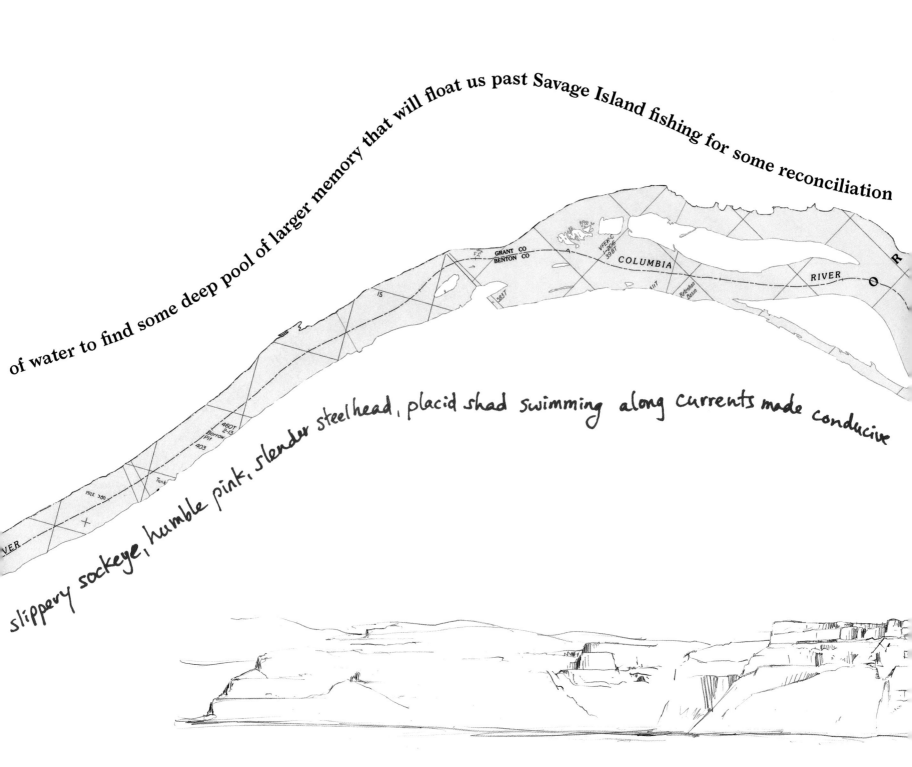

of water to find some deep pool of larger memory that will float us past Savage Island fishing for some reconciliation

slippery sockeye, humble pink, slender steelhead, placid shad swimming along currents made conducive

with the Osprey and the Cutthroat this neighbourhood's too busy we've parked this nightmare all over Isla Tortuga

by beaver dams water striders above depths of mouthy bass, walleye, catfish in the reach & leak of

COLUMBIA 34

COLUMBIA RIVER

COLUMBIA FRANKLIN CO BENTON CO RIVER FRANK BENTO

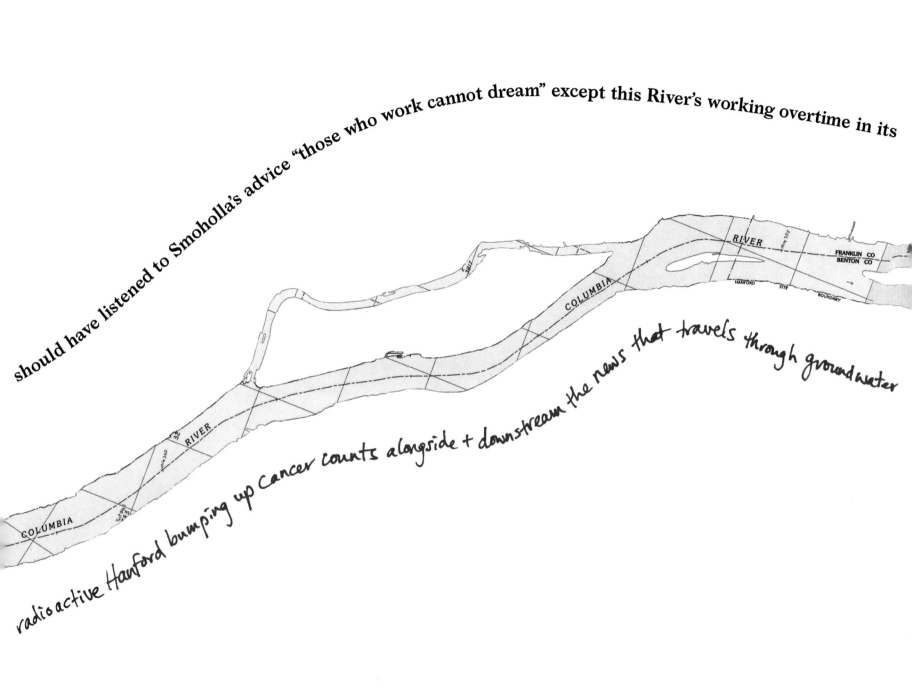

should have listened to Smoholla's advice "those who work cannot dream" except this River's working overtime in its

radioactive Hanford bumping up cancer counts alongside + downstream the news that travels through groundwater go-with-the-flow M.O. and its maximum flow efficiency is always channel-hopping it's not the map of our

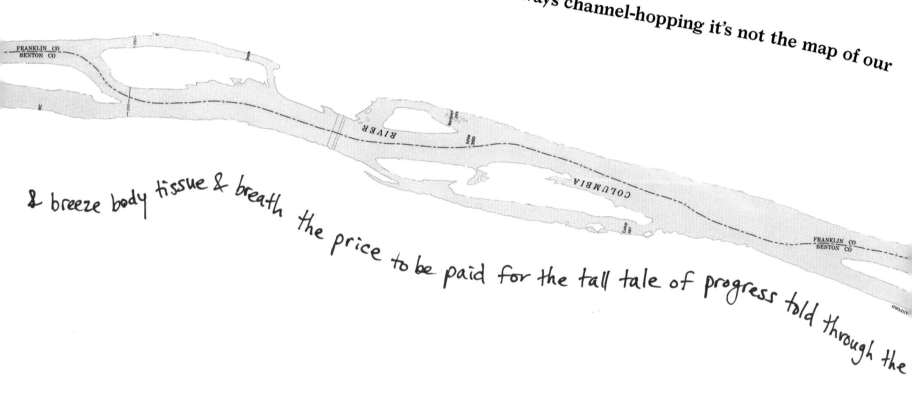

& breeze body tissue & breath the price to be paid for the tall tale of progress told through the

street of dreams subtract the cities the neighbour's waterline blurs the other shore the forked tongue slurs the

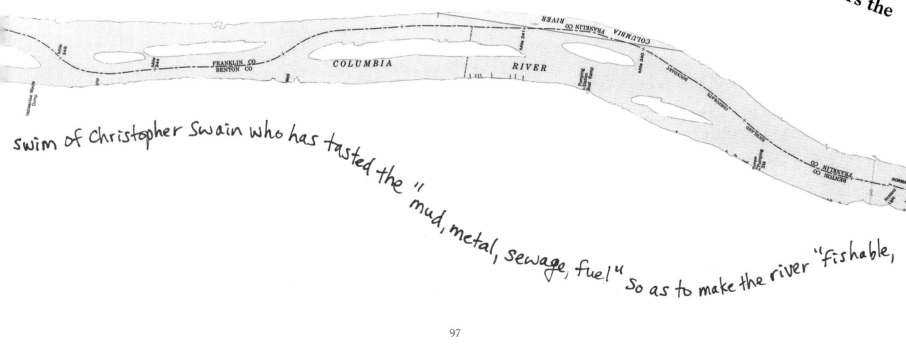

swim of Christopher Swain who has tasted the "mud, metal, sewage, fuel" so as to make the river "fishable,

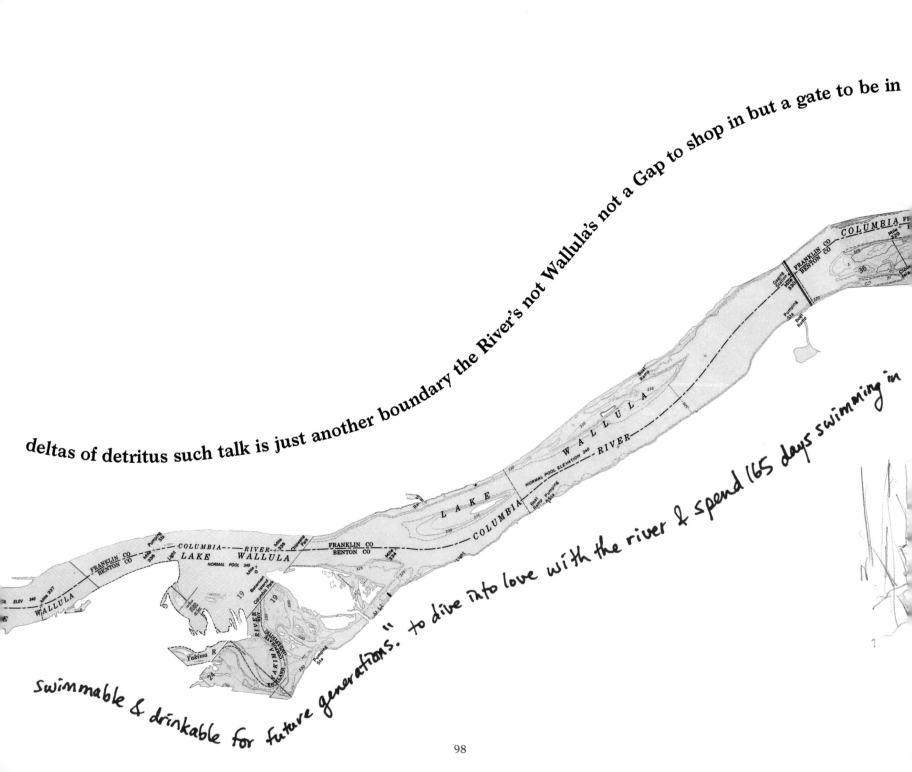

deltas of detritus such talk is just another boundary the River's not Wallula's not a Gap to shop in but a gate to be in

swimmable & drinkable for future generations." to dive into love with the river & spend 165 days swimming in

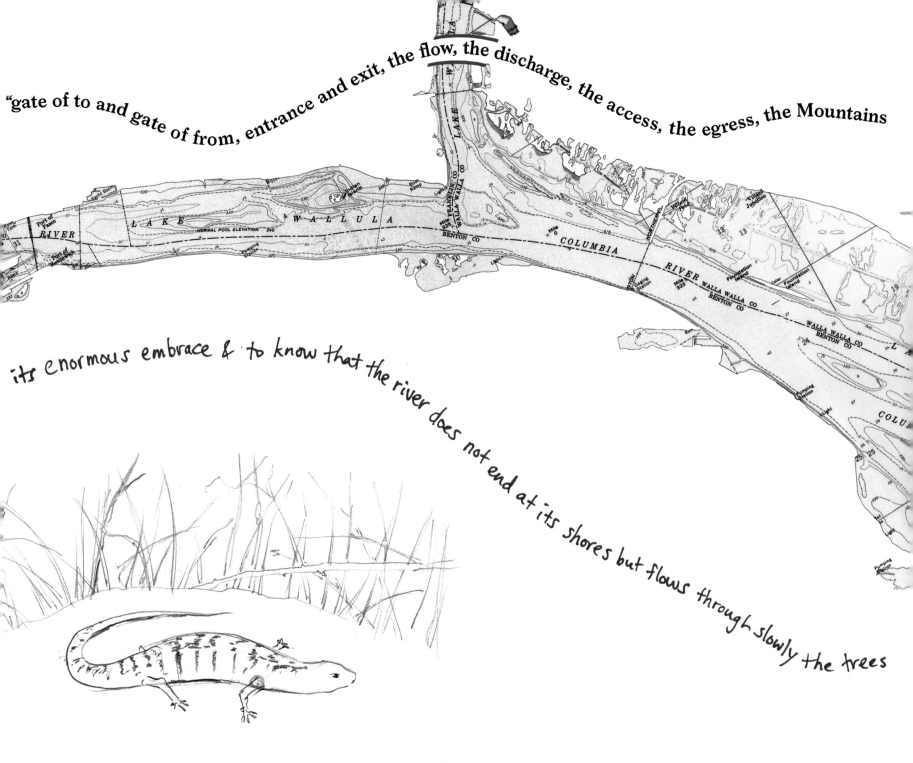

"gate of to and gate of from, entrance and exit, the flow, the discharge, the access, the egress, the Mountains

its enormous embrace & to know that the river does not end at its shores but flows through slowly the trees

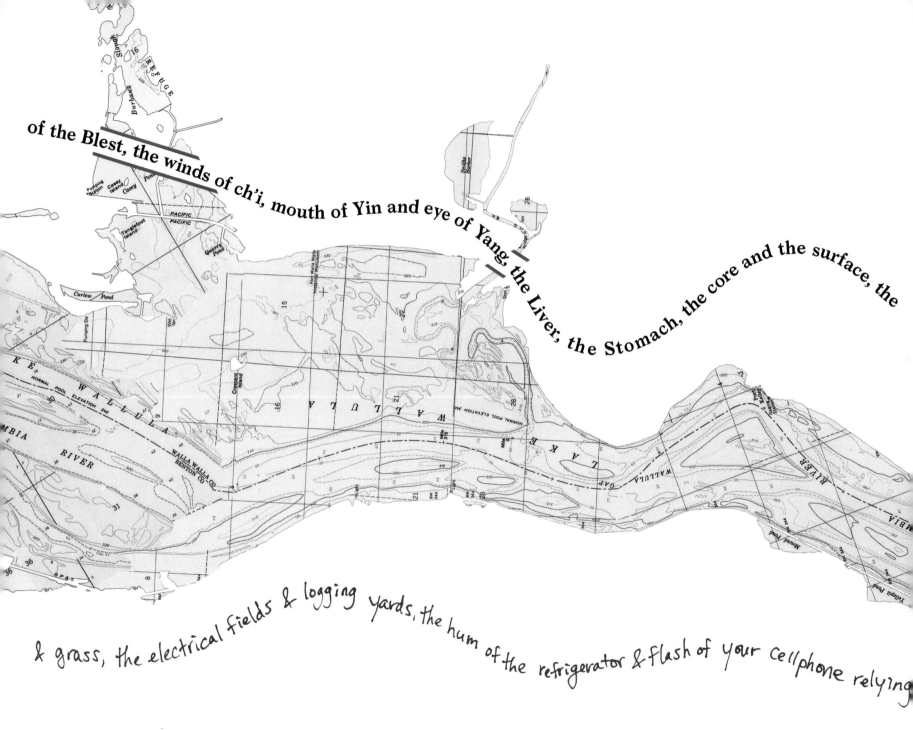

of the Blest, the winds of ch'i, mouth of Yin and eye of Yang, the Liver, the Stomach, the core and the surface, the

& grass, the electrical fields & logging yards, the hum of the refrigerator & flash of your cellphone relying

rock and the lake. These are the gates and you can either kick them open or walk through in silence. Same dif."

on river whether you know it or not, river as archive of rain, pesticides, urban debris,

Inside out this basalt lava bends into water shears and folds beneath this border bridge hello Rita nice to see

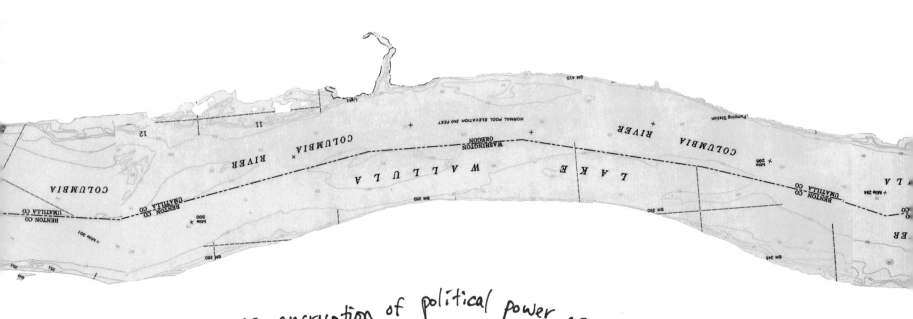

rural runoff river as encryption of political power as exodus of endangered species

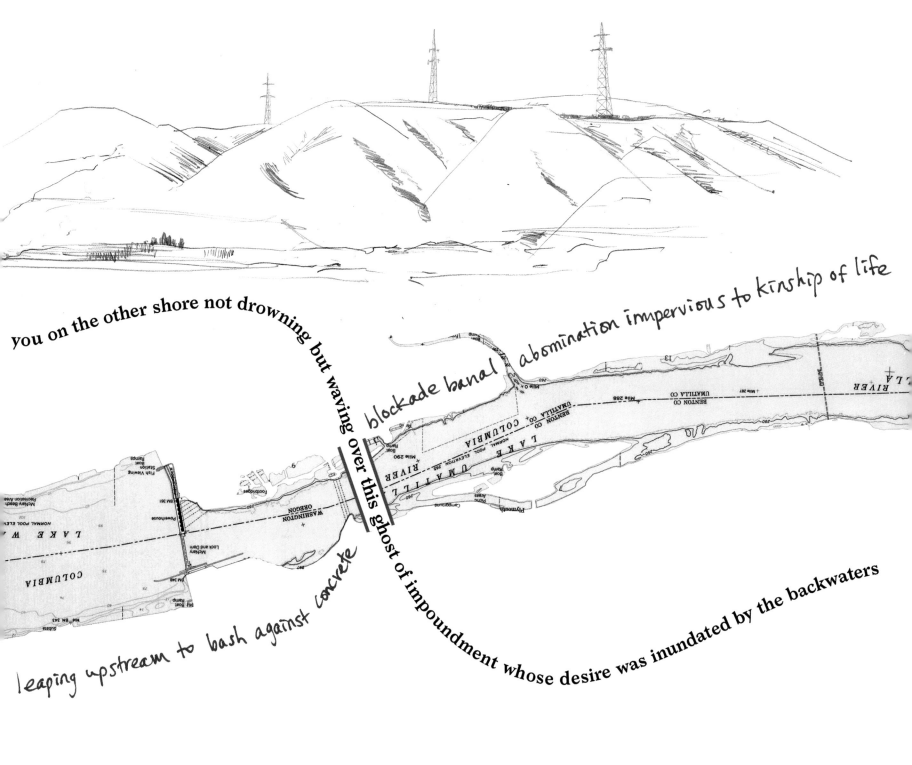

you on the other shore not drowning but waving over this ghost of impoundment whose desire was inundated by the backwaters

blockade banal abomination impervious to kinship of life

leaping upstream to bash against concrete

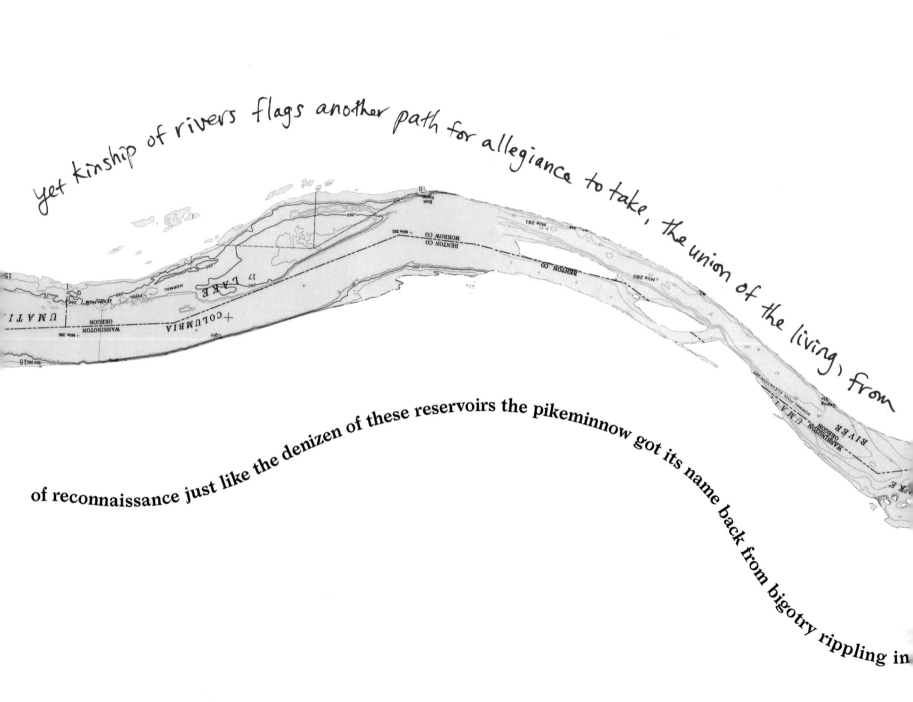

yet kinship of rivers flags another path for allegiance to take, the union of the living, from

of reconnaissance just like the denizen of these reservoirs the pikeminnow got its name back from bigotry rippling in

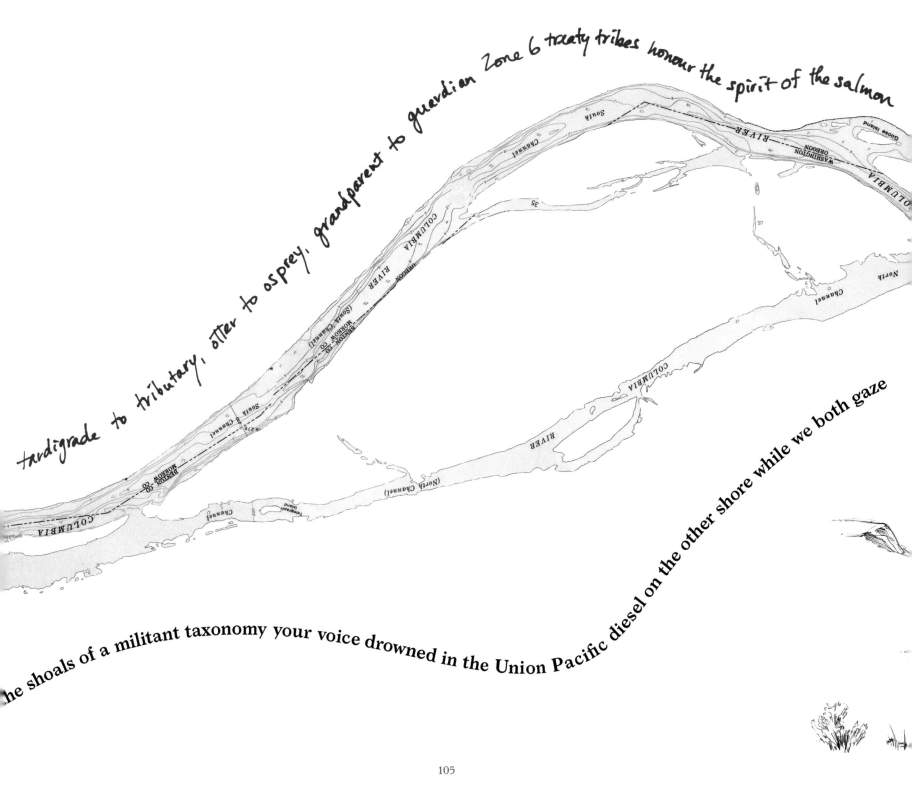

tardigrade to tributary, otter to osprey, grandparent to guardian Zone 6 treaty tribes honour the spirit of the salmon

while we both gaze

the shoals of a militant taxonomy your voice drowned in the Union Pacific diesel on the other shore

Inter-Tribal Fish Commission put fish back into rivers & protect watersheds, brace for climate destabilization

at this water for the ear of the other and meditate the forgotten thinking of the River's language not its meaning petroglyphs watch over the efforts it's very late but not too late for environmental justice "whether

after all but how to dive through its unthought surface into the deep "as is" or was always minding its own

they realize it or not, every single person in the Northwest is a Wy-Kan-Ush-Pum. We are all Salmon People!

anyness a vocabulary of leftovers in the mud a polluted memory of its pure Kootenay percolation part of the same

Nch'i Wàna's Confederated Tribes pull together across the state line that divides Washington from Oregon,

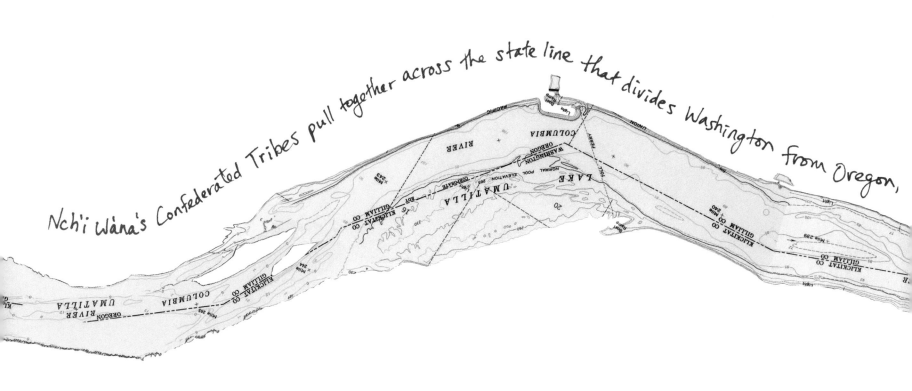

beaver system fur quivering now seems as clear as the imaginary state line that runs down the middle affirming

floating or submerged by the river. another reservoir misnamed as lake. 1971. locked into logic of highway

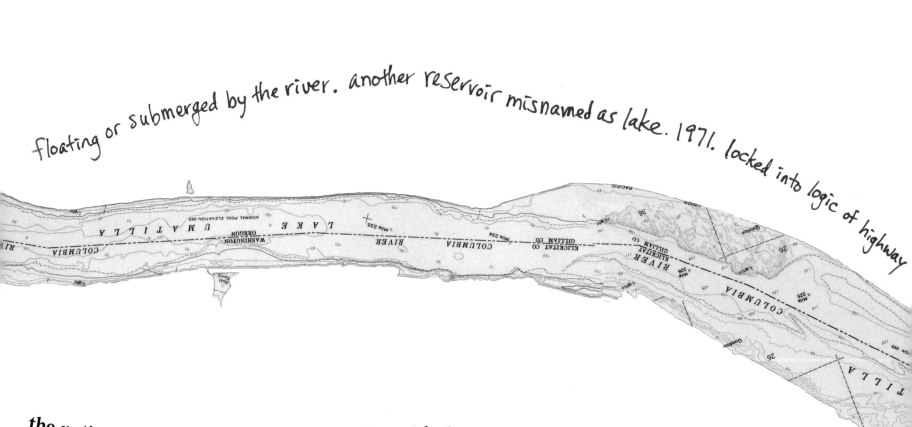

the nation's strength and infinite possibility with the clues of Missoula spread out for the eye another power

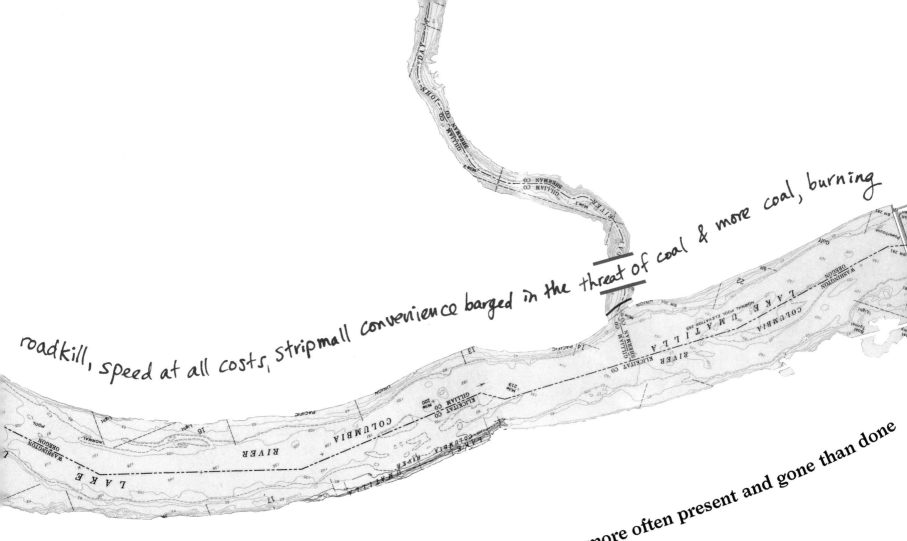

roadkill, speed at all costs, stripmall convenience barged in the threat of coal & more coal, burning

magic the River reveres or something like a ferry over shining water more often present and gone than done

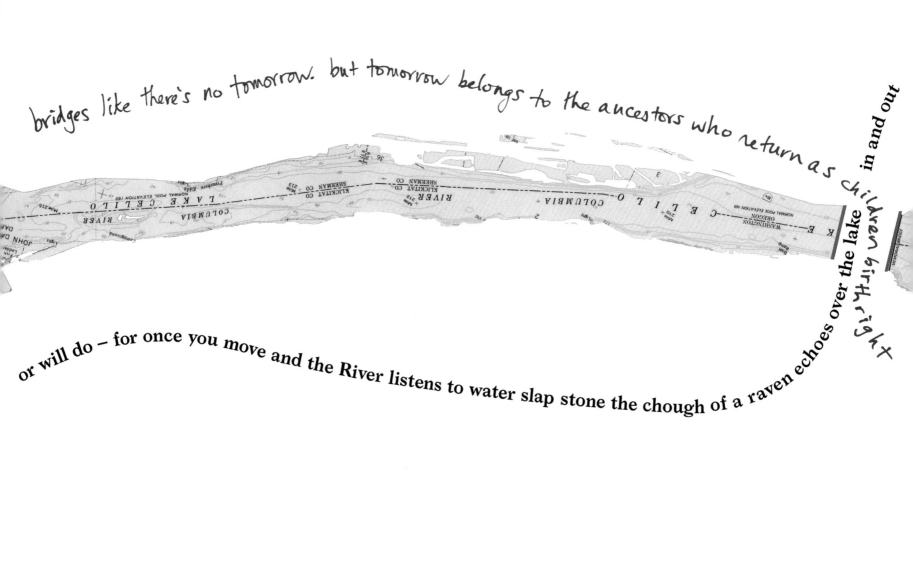

bridges like there's no tomorrow. but tomorrow belongs to the ancestors who return as children birthright in and out

or will do – for once you move and the River listens to water slap stone the chough of a raven echoes over the lake the afternoon shadows lengthen across the River a truck moves above the silent echo of Wyam Falls the unthought

to live on this earth with dignity, to swim river, not slackwater, to sing the river's songs.

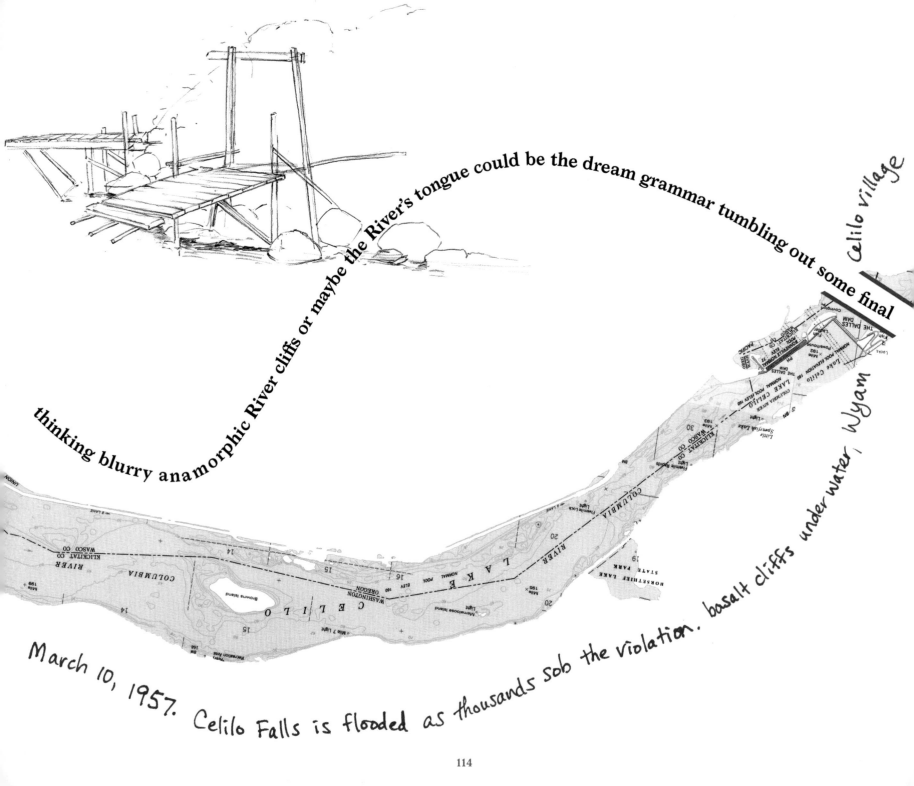

thinking blurry anamorphic River cliffs or maybe the River's tongue could be the dream grammar tumbling out some final

Celilo village

basalt cliffs under water, Wyam

March 10, 1957. Celilo Falls is flooded as thousands sob the violation.

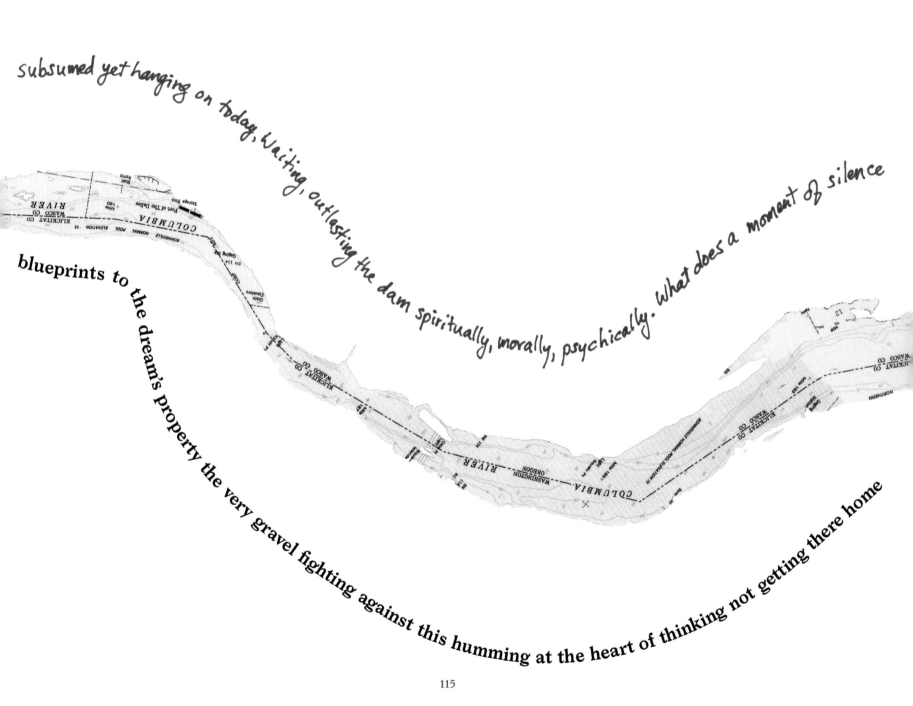

subsumed yet hanging on today, waiting, outlasting the dam spiritually, morally, psychically. What does a moment of silence

blueprints to the dream's property the very gravel fighting against this humming at the heart of thinking not getting there home

in 2007 by Oregon's senators mean? What does the lengthening silence of the falls mean? Why keep listening?

again home again to the storm of the ear that stellar steering of the passage junction box genetic feeding at the creek

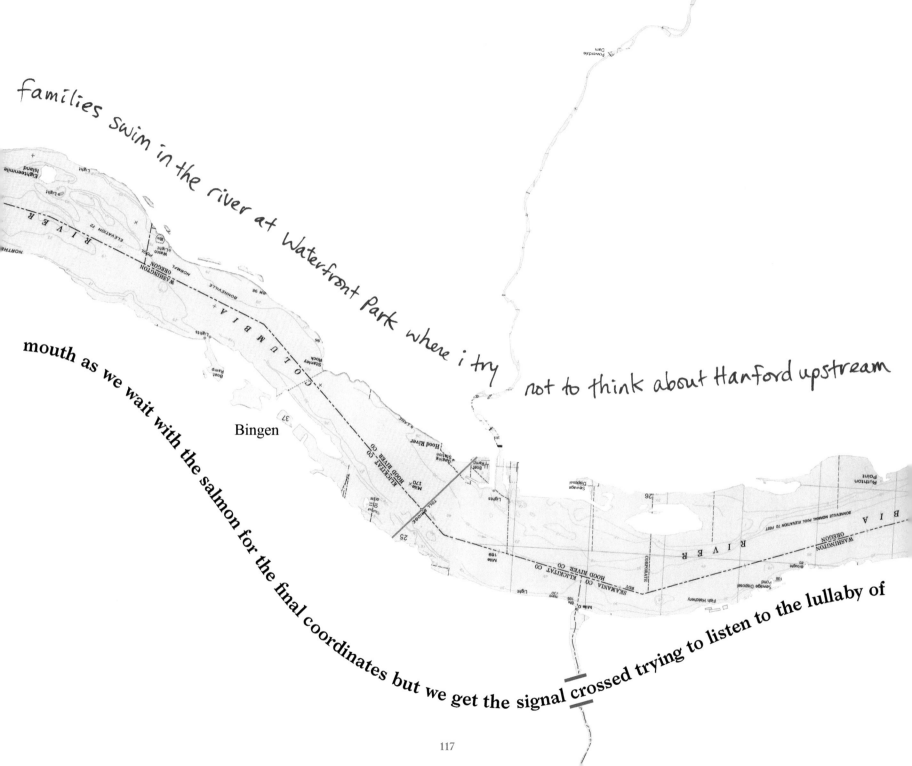

families swim in the river at Waterfront Park where i try

not to think about Hanford upstream

mouth as we wait with the salmon for the final coordinates but we get the signal crossed trying to listen to the lullaby of

Bingen

windsurfers help us to see air's power with each leap, swoop & veer learning to see the unseen below

Wah Gwin Gwin Falls and continue to displace the lexicon of water with the grammar of hearing when I will

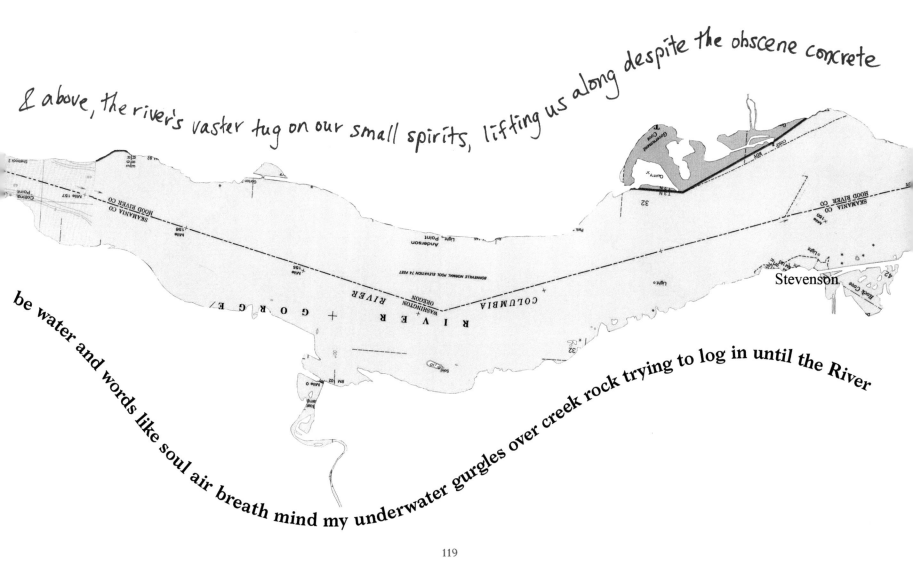

& above, the river's vaster tug on our small spirits, lifting us along despite the obscene concrete

be water and words like soul air breath mind my underwater gurgles over creek rock trying to log in until the River

Stevenson

that slows the water's rush & speeds mass extinction trophic cascade, how many generations?

sounds like a Sunday drive as it feeds itself into its own moan aligned with body fallen flowed down mouth the way the

to reach & reach, for what? the water slips through your fingers but teaches temperature,

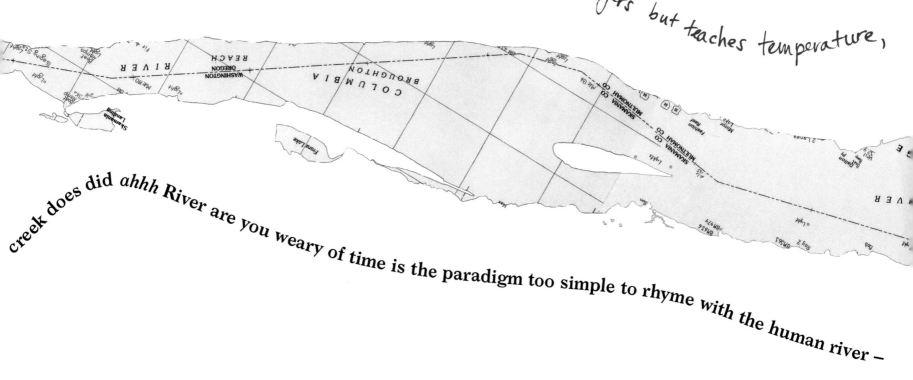

creek does did *ahhh* **River** are you weary of time is the paradigm too simple to rhyme with the human river —

turbidity, toxicity through touch what is missing? unseen under the highway's roar? the

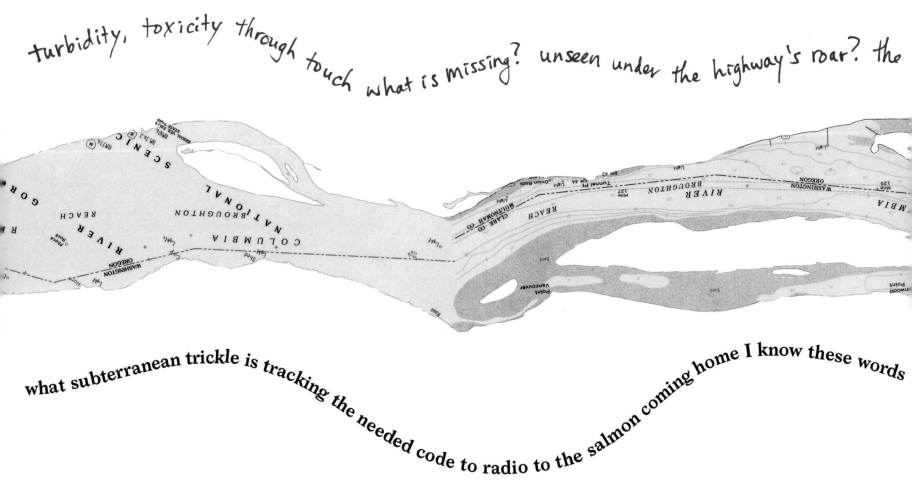

what subterranean trickle is tracking the needed code to radio to the salmon coming home I know these words

Sandy River Bird Blind tells me: bats, bobcats, marmots, ermine, mountain goats & much more,

just turn you into metaphor, rock of ages how to defend you and me from a language edited as news do those

can the Confluence Project help us to return some homelands to those who've been pushed out?

deer swimming the rock-wall river mean anything beyond the barge is not the River's voice its government an our lives depend upon it

island standing in the way a crow pecking plastic from the dumpster behind Taco Bell just off the I-5 the River's voice ignores the quiet

so i visit Powell's Books to find How To Save a River (How to Save Ourselves), Dam

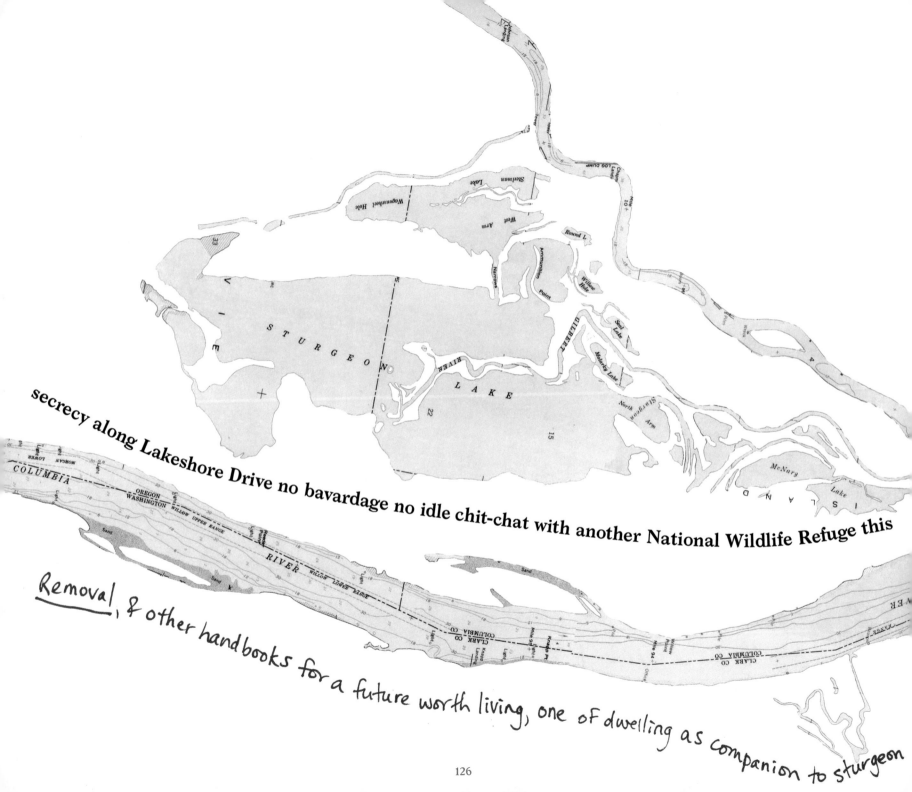

secrecy along Lakeshore Drive no bavardage no idle chit-chat with another National Wildlife Refuge this

Removal, & other handbooks for a future worth living, one of dwelling as companion to sturgeon mighty voice refuses to negotiate but sings a little harmony under the squealing wheels of the Portland &

Wanapum and   all the river's   peoples practicing   the art of enough, after the excess has

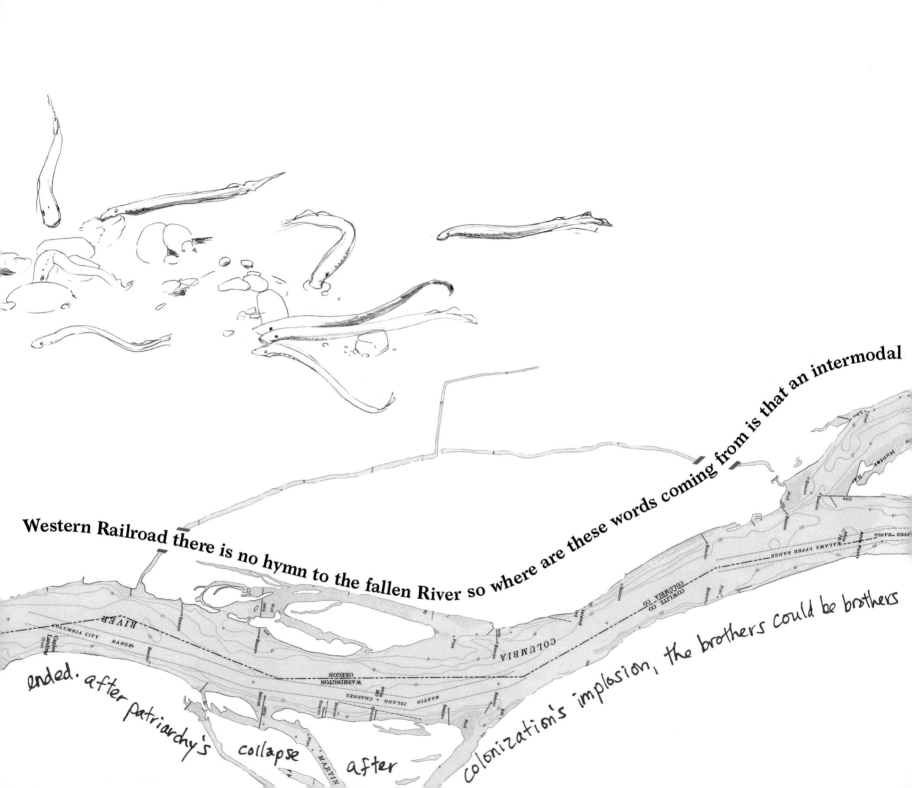

Western Railroad there is no hymn to the fallen River so where are these words coming from is that an intermodal

ended. after patriarchy's collapse after colonization's implosion, the brothers could be brothers

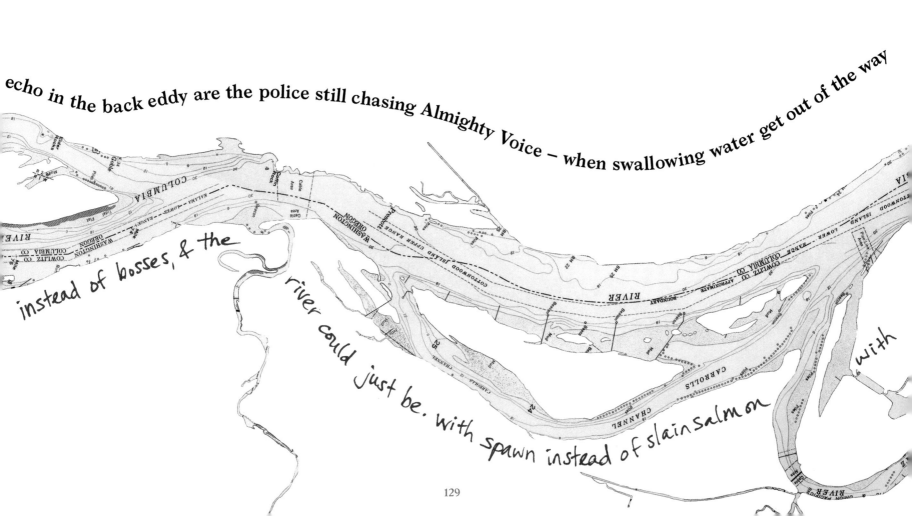

echo in the back eddy are the police still chasing Almighty Voice – when swallowing water get out of the way

instead of bosses, & the river could just be. with spawn instead of slain salmon with

129

when the line disappears talk to the hook by now we know you're not pure and you just make it up sometimes

a dignity that cannot be taken away, not by the buzz of wires, not by the hum of highway, not by

COLUMBIA RIVER

RIVER

WASHINGTON
OREGON

WASHINGTON
OREGON

COLUMBIA CO
COWLITZ CO

CHANNEL

SLAUGHTERS

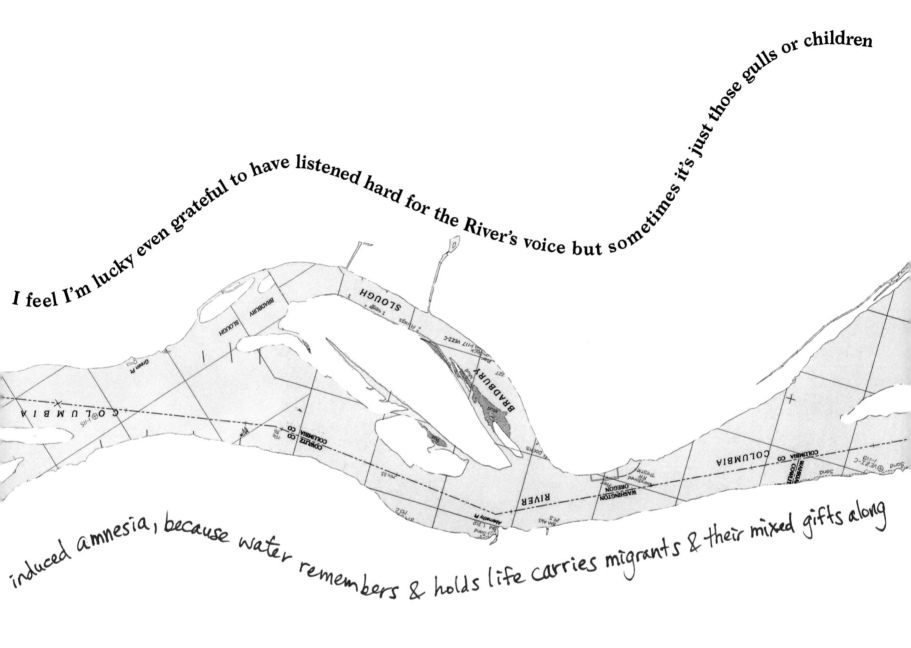

I feel I'm lucky even grateful to have listened hard for the River's voice but sometimes it's just those gulls or children

induced amnesia, because water remembers & holds life carries migrants & their mixed gifts along

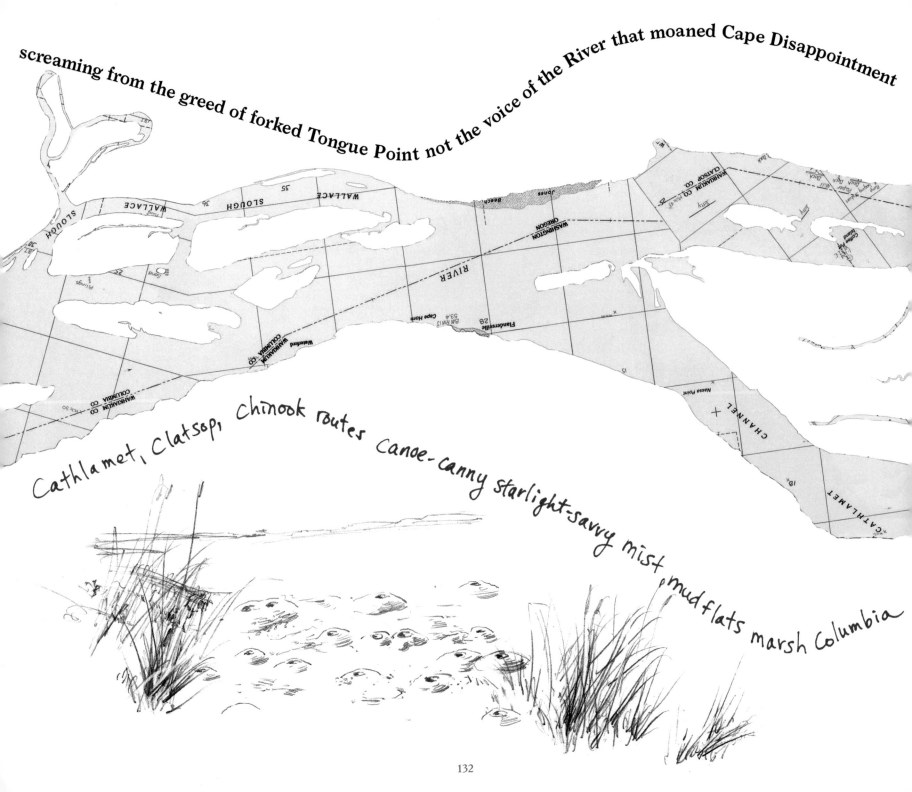

screaming from the greed of forked Tongue Point not the voice of the River that moaned Cape Disappointment

Cathlamet, Clatsop, Chinook routes canoe-canny starlight-savvy mist mudflats marsh Columbia

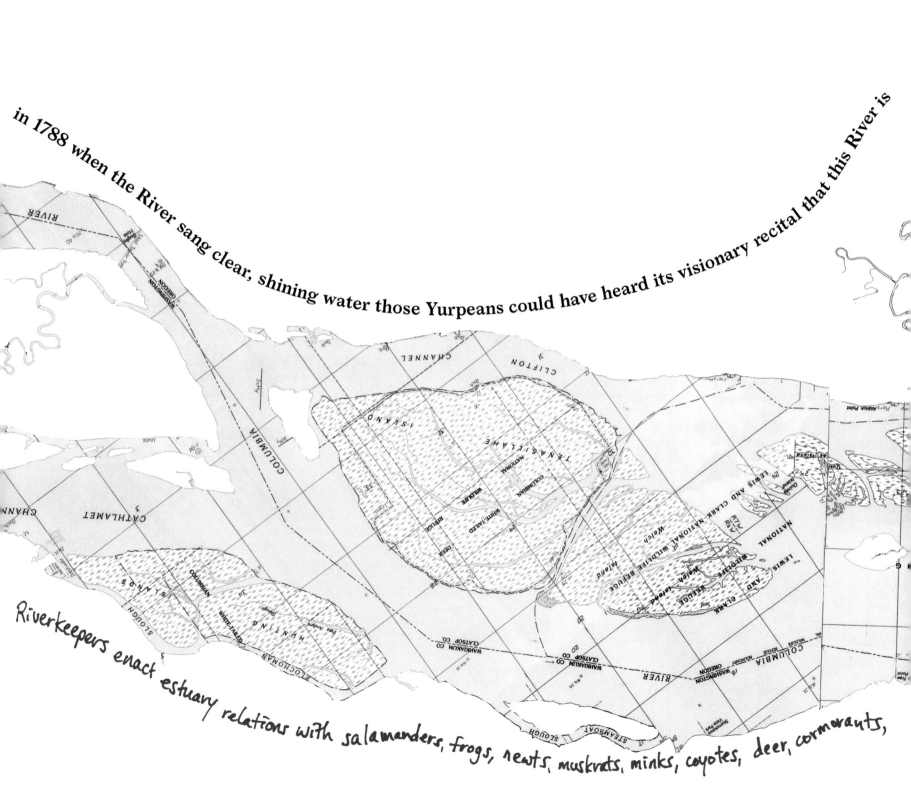

in 1788 when the River sang clear, shining water those Yurpeans could have heard its visionary recital that this River is

Riverkeepers enact estuary relations with salamanders, frogs, newts, muskrats, minks, coyotes, deer, cormorants,

the way home the return to what we have left that this is the place where I come from I was on my way to

grebes, gulls, herons, geese, eagles, soaring over Sitka spruce, willow, cottonwood, wapato, camas tongued in chinookan

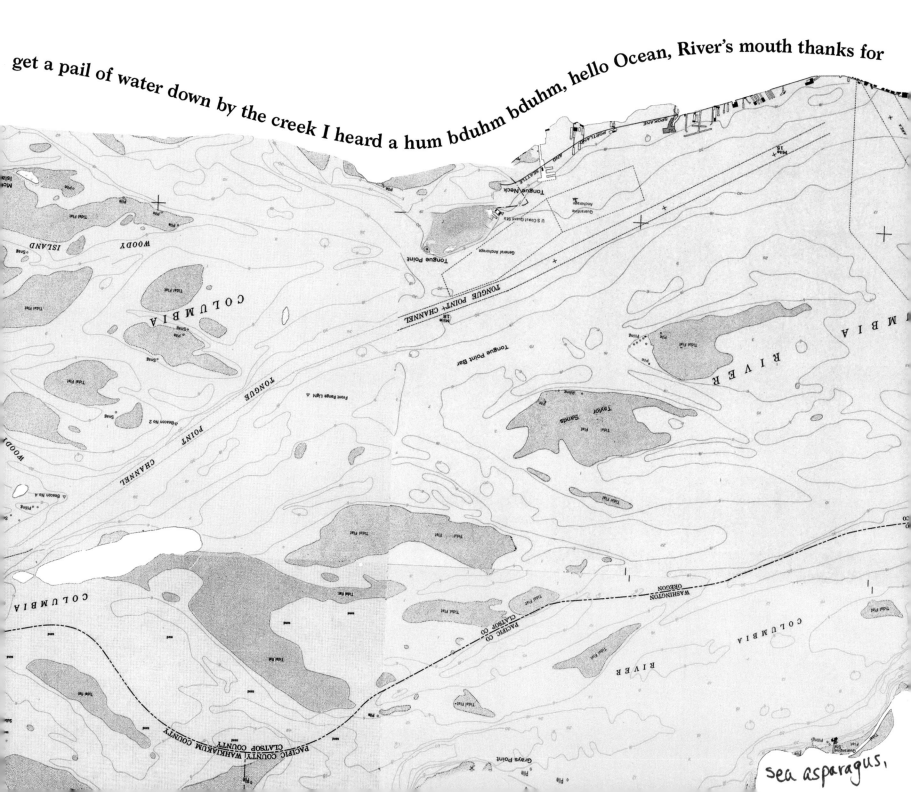

get a pail of water down by the creek I heard a hum bduhm bduhm, hello Ocean, River's mouth thanks for

sea asparagus,

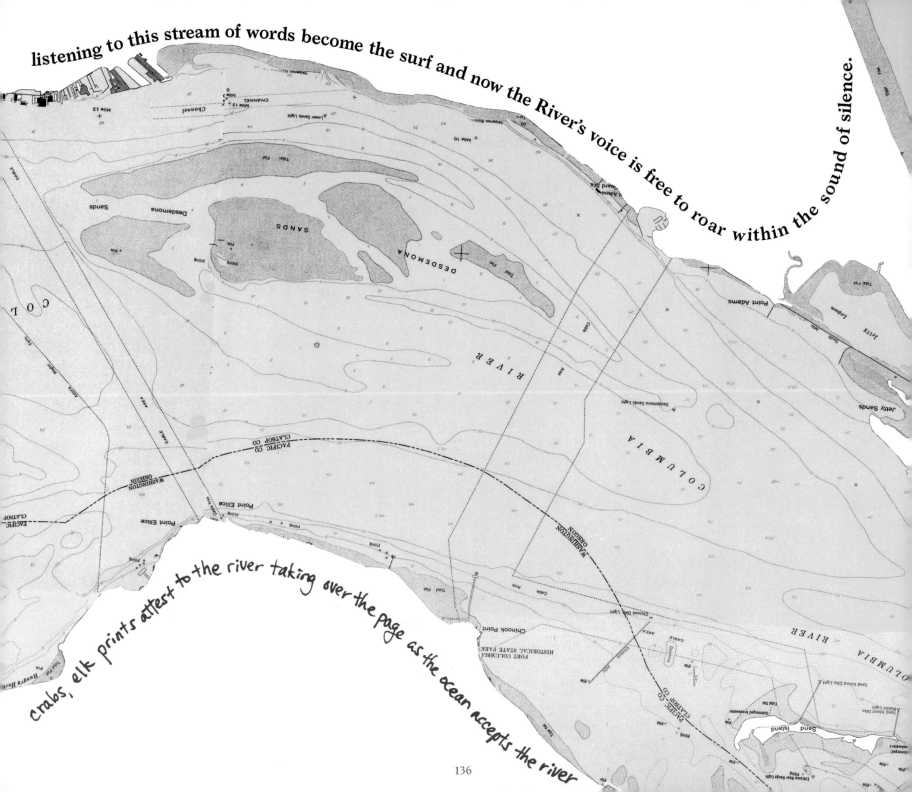

listening to this stream of words become the surf and now the River's voice is free to roar within the sound of silence.

crabs, elk prints attest to the river taking over the page as the ocean accepts the river

136

PACIFIC

DUMP SITE

DUMP SITE

PROJECT DEPTH 14.6 METERS (48 ft)

JETTY

COLUMBIA RIVER

COLUMBIA RIVER

Mile 4

WASHINGTON
OREGON

Mile 0

Submerged Breakwaters

Tidal Flat

Piling

Tidal Flat

Submerged Breakwater

Dolphin

Afterwords, a Dialogue

FRED WAH – Where did the words come from for what we were doing with the Columbia River?

RITA WONG – Maybe the River gifted us those words. That said, I also feel the limits of my English filter, and I would like to start by recognizing the long-term, existing nations, cultures, languages, and relationships along the river, as it flows through and shapes the traditional, unceded territories of the Indigenous Peoples along the length of the Columbia River watershed, including but not limited to the: ʔakisq̓nuk, Kenpésq̓, Shuswap, Ktunaxa, Sinixt, Secwepemc, Okanagan, the Confederated Tribes of the Colville Reservation (Colville, Nespelem, Sanpoil, Palus, Wenatchi, Chelan, Entiat, Methow, Southern Okonogan, Moses Columbia, Nez Perce), Wanapum, Kalispel, Kootenai, Salish, Flathead, Coeur d'Alene, Colville, Spokane, Umatilla, Yakama, Burns Paiute, Paiute Shoshone, Shoshone-Bannock, Warm Springs, Nez Perce, Chinook, Cowlitz, Lake, Sanpoil, Columbia, Wasco-Wishram, Tlatskanai, and Clatsop.

   While I'm deeply grateful for what I learned from journeying along the river at different times, I need to be clear that there is so much more I do not know. Despite the effects of the dams which amount to attempted genocide, I hope to witness a resurgence of Indigenous Peoples and languages along the river because this is good for everyone and necessary if humanity wants to remain on this planet. I believe in the principle that has been attributed to Lilla Watson and Aboriginal activists in Australia, who said, "If you have come here to help me, you are wasting your time. But if you have come here because your liberation is bound up with mine, then let us work together" (Watson, quoted in K. Faith and K. Pate, p. 147). How can we work with the river and its peoples through whatever skills and capacities we happen to carry?

FRED – I found in approaching our project, after we had decided to do this poem as long as the river, that I had to first shed my preconceptions, not about the river, but about what I could bring to the river. One of the greatest experiences of making this composition was finding out that I had to listen to the river to hear what resonations were available. You're right. Language was something that bounced back from the river. I know you've done a lot of writing on water, and thinking with water generally, not just the river. You came to this project with a sense of water.

RITA – Water is infused throughout everything, everyone. We're two-thirds water. While we're talking about the river, it's not just the river that ends at its banks. It's the river that powers our cellphones, it's the river that allows for the birds and the fish, all the people who rely on all that the river enlivens, all of it, that's the river too. When we're talking about water, we're also talking about land, and we're also talking about our bodies and ourselves. A lot of it is unconscious.

I don't know that I came to this project with many preconceptions. I think I came with a sense of openness and just trying to pay attention. Though this is a watershed I did not grow up in, I've still been relying on it whether I knew it or not. And connected to it, against its will in some ways, and maybe against my will too, but nonetheless that relationship exists.

FRED — What do you mean, "against your will"?

RITA — I don't want to be benefitting from the fourteen dams along the Columbia River and the electric power that comes from those hydro dams. I don't want to be using that energy. I understand that it has caused massive devastation, that it has choked or ended incredible salmon runs, and almost driven Indigenous Peoples to the brink of genocide. It's only due to their resilience that they're still there. They're still there and they're fighting to uphold their sacred relationships with the salmon and to return the river back to health. When I think about all those things, I don't want to be using the electricity from those dams. I understand that I need electricity and I'll have to use it at some point, but I'd rather figure other ways to do that, and I'd rather figure out ways to decrease my use of electricity. It's not a system I chose to be plugged into but I am plugged into it, and I have to figure out how to deal with that. When I visit the river, it's with that history. I don't find ideas around guilt to be useful. I think questions of responsibility are more helpful in thinking it through, because I don't want to be stuck in this place of paralysis or fearfulness. I just want to see what's there, and I want to figure out how to respond to it. In the present. Given all the historical devastation, all the trauma, all the violence, all of

that, we're still here and we have a responsibility to respond to it. I was really stunned by how incredible that river is. When we visited headwaters, for instance, how humble, how simple, how incredibly beautiful the beginning of that river is.

FRED — Yes, just a spring out of the ground at the head of Columbia Lake.

RITA — And by the time you get to the river's mouth near Astoria, it's incredible. What happened from here to there? It's so amazing to see the river is five miles wide at its mouth. The river is full of surprise and wonder. It's this sacred being.

FRED — This complicity you have with the river and its power, was this one of the reasons you chose to handwrite your poem rather than type it?

RITA — I just had a feeling that I wanted to stay with the hand, with the flow, with the body. And the composition of writing something along the whole length of the map of the river, the representation of the river, not the river itself, I felt like I had to sit down and have long stretches of time just returning to where we were and trying to write through and around and over and under those moments. It's sort of an unusual, for me anyway, compositional process in the sense of trying to write as long as I could, stay with the length and the flow of it.

FRED — I don't think I was as engaged with the "difficulties" around the river as you were, although I recognized them. One of the great things for me about doing this project with you, although we didn't use the poems as conversation, was just being around one another and talking, so I became more aware of some of your concerns, what I thought of as the "difficulties." But the "difficulties" that we encounter going down the river, you know, like seeing a logging truck, seeing the diesel train, the tracks going alongside the river because the river has given them this graded bed of travel, those were always in my mind. And those "difficulties" kept coming up in language. For example, the word diesel. When we were out on Lake Windermere and saw the Canadian Pacific coal cars along the tracks, suddenly we heard that incredible noise of the diesel engines disturbing this beautiful marshland. Getting that word diesel was a gift of the occasion. It's kind of like a knock on the door, "Oh diesel," the implications of power and oil. All of a sudden there's this large resonation out into the world, of the river, and of course it is a mighty river. It has all kinds of industrial, agricultural, hydropower – there's a whole bunch of ramifications that you can't resist. For me, the language keeps coming out of such "difficulties." In another sense, as I think most of us have experienced in trying to get close to the river, it is the body, touch, and sensation, that sense of the materiality of the river itself. Looking for language that represents that materiality, finding words for the surface of the water, the depth of the water, the things in the water, was a constant awareness. To me it was one of the most amazing compositional experiences I've had in my writing life. Though we had agreed to do this project, I didn't know how we were going to get to the end of this long river. As you say, the writing was a gift of language, but also discovering the language that one could work with there. I kept thinking of that sense from Allen Ginsberg's long poem "Wichita Vortex Sutra" of looking for the right language. A kind of ethical responsibility to look for the right language; responsibility, respect, paying attention to its history, paying attention to where the river is in terms of people, their own industry along the river. One of the things that I wasn't able to get at with the river is what's underneath the surface. I felt I can only go so far and the river has more down there than I can deal with.

RITA – Even when we're talking about the diesel moment, and it was loud, the words that come to me when I remember being in that lake, are actually tule and bulrush, the little bits of life that have been there longer than that diesel train, and will be there much longer after that diesel train. And what you call the "difficulties" I think of, partly, as the "debt." Maybe another way of thinking about it if we're talking about gifts is that if a gift is given to me, I feel an urge to reciprocate. "What's the best gift you have to give back" may be another way of thinking about it.

FRED – What would that be?

RITA – I think it starts by paying attention and being present. I feel that needs to be in coordination with a lot of other things. We're in this historical moment with this possible Columbia River Treaty negotiation, so it would be doing whatever we can to support the Indigenous Peoples' efforts to help the salmon return, to get ecosystems valued as much as everything else on that river. To me that would be a form of giving back that has an impact for future generations and would make a difference for somebody else besides me.

FRED – Then how does your poem give back?

RITA — I think it's part of the process of coming to terms with what you're part of, whether you like it or not. I don't know if it gives back or not. I certainly hope that it does by encouraging people to consider their relationships with the river, to responsibly care for the river and its life. But that remains to be seen. A shift in consciousness needs to be materialized through changes in behaviour and actions that actually work to regenerate life with the river.

FRED — My experience with giving back, or being present, was one of the big jolts I had in writing this project. You know I grew up along that water system. I was teaching at Selkirk College in the late sixties, early seventies when they were dislocating these communities along the Arrow Lakes. There were some protests and I wasn't really engaged. In fact there wasn't much "activism" in the community around that. It was during the Vietnam War and that was the big political thing. I'm really surprised that I was there, and this was going on and I didn't realize it for close to fifty years. I had not paid any attention to where I was at that time. Going back, coming to the river now, in the twenty-first century, that sort of stunned me, it raised my consciousness about the river, about what building dams and reservoirs does to people. I'm certainly going to be more of a voice for that when I can be. But I also want to somehow put trust in my poem to last through, be there for others. It was certainly there for myself, in terms of addressing some of the difficulties. That comes up a lot in your writing. Your acute attention to the Indigeneity along the river, the fact the river was so much a part of these Indigenous Nations for so long and still matters in so many ways. And that a lot of the language that they come to the river with is worth paying attention to, needs to be paid attention to.

RITA — Like when we stopped at the Wanapum Heritage Centre. That Centre is incredibly moving, the kind of consciousness and story that people are living out and carrying forward. For me, that was one of the highlights of that trip. The Wanapum are surrounded in all directions, by nuclear waste from the Hanford Site on one side, dam on the other side, corporate orchards, huge apple orchards on the other side. Every direction is this intense, violent exploitation, and yet they're still there and they're still connected to the river. That's amazing to me, that kind of relationship to place and home.

FRED — Or that day we were in Grand Coulee, this huge megaproject in upstate Washington, and you and I walked across the bridge and up to the Colville Tribal Museum, and heard the story from that point of view. Most people driving through Grand Coulee don't get that.

RITA — They miss such important parts of the place. The museum, the bookstore, the woman at the bookstore was incredibly knowledgeable. So much depth there.

In terms of whether the poem lasts through or whether it has a future life, I don't know, I feel like we're in a society that needs a paradigm shift, and if we make it through the paradigm shift there'll be readers down the road for this poem. I don't know if we're going to make it through the paradigm shift. I really hope we do. But it feels to me like a very dangerous or precarious time that we're living through, and I actually don't know where we're going to end up, or make it through as a species. Regardless, I think, back to that question of reciprocity, what do you have to give or what do you have to pay attention to? I think it comes back to the river itself, for me. There's a lot of noise around that river, a lot of mess, and damage. But there's still this incredible river. It's bloated in places beyond recognition. To me it feels tortured.

FRED — Well, most of it isn't a river anymore, it's a reservoir. Big lakes of water that aren't moving very quickly.

RITA — But then you get to Astoria and you see elk prints near the mouth of the river.

FRED — One of the things that I stumbled upon while working on this: I was always very impressed by those videos about the Missoula Floods, thousands of years ago. We were driving along the river and looking at these erratics, these boulders that were part of that, way out in some field. And I started thinking about that sense of "deep time," that we're just a pinhead in this whole thing.

RITA — That's what I think about the tules. For me that diesel's a moment of noise and then it's over.

FRED — This whole sense, in writing about the river, of our own involvement at this point in deep time, is not meaningless but so minuscule that, in a sense, the poem almost feels petty.

RITA — It's a trickle in the context of that much larger river. It's good for poetry to be humble about itself.

FRED — But it also brought me back to that sense of awe. I think we got that out of Peter Warshall's wonderful essay on water.

RITA — "Watershed Governance: Checklists to Encourage Respect for Waterflows and People."

FRED — That water is itself, water is its own being. Both through Peter Warshall's essay and also Jeannette Armstrong's "the great River   as is" in her poem "Water is Siwlkw," that whole sense of the isness of the river.

RITA — I come to that through the Coast Salish writer Lee Maracle as well, when she says the water owns itself in her contribution to the *downstream: reimagining water* anthology (Wilfrid Laurier University Press, 2017).

FRED — I was brought back to that sense of the Tao, you know, "That which exists through itself is what is called Meaning" (Richard Wilhelm, *The Secret of the Golden Flower*). The thing that exists is itself. That's what we need to pay attention to, is the thing itself. That whole sense of isness, metaphysically, philosophically, poetically, really engaged me. I've always known about it, but then I thought of this river as its own isness. That relieved me of having to write "about" the river, and I felt more comfortable about simply being with it. And a lot of times in the poem, for me, it became a playful experience.
    What else?

RITA — It's a long river.

FRED — Yes, it's such a material thing, it's water, it has banks, it has history, the long time of itself, like the Missoula Floods, and it's still there, this water flowing out to the Pacific Ocean. We have to imagine that maybe someday that water's not going to be there. It brought me back to what I sometimes think of as the proprioceptive quality of experience. So that the words in the poem have substance. I've often thought what I really want to do is print out each of these words that I've put here beside the river on pieces of wood and float them down the river.

RITA – That'd be so much fun. Let's do it. We need to ask permission of the river first.

FRED – Do you have any sense of that concern I've had, of what's underneath the surface? Do you have any sense of the non-human aspects of the river?

RITA – Well, the big one is fish.

FRED – But we didn't go fishing.

RITA – At one point we were looking for fish in the river, maybe around the Lardeau River.

FRED – Right, looking for the rainbow trout who spawn in that river.

RITA – Yet I feel there are so many other lives in the watershed and so many other people who are knowledgeable in different ways. Going back to feeling humble; the smallness of the poem in contrast to the largeness of the watershed. I would love it if other people would consider doing that kind of journey, just spending time with the river, and see what they generated from it, how they would give back to the river through words or creative acts. Like a fisher

would come up with a very different rendering: it might be a song, it might be a sculpture, who knows. I think there's a value and a wonderfulness to spend time with the river, at a moment when we're being asked to pay attention to so many other things, so much noise, so much speed, so much social media. Just being able to have the gift of paying attention with and to the river, for even a few days at a stretch. That's what we shouldn't lose sight of.

FRED – One of the things that was going on for me, as a kind of an offshoot of the river was the question of "treaty." And particularly here in Canada the question of "treatied" and "untreatied" territory has come up. I got into this track of researching Indigenous notions of treaty. Particularly in regard to the notion that a treaty works both ways, that we also have an obligation to the treaty. We so frequently see treaty as being something for "them."

RITA – But those who hold "Canadian" citizenship are bound by it, whether they understand this or not.

FRED – And then what I got interested in was the whole notion of protocol around treaty from an Indigenous point of view. So that was something I learned, that word treaty, and the implications around the fact that the river is involved in the Columbia River Treaty, between two nations and a province. I think, as settlers or unsettlers, we're not really looking at that treaty in the right way. Fully. If one engaged the proper protocols, we would treat it quite differently. So I was interested in writing the poem that way, I had to listen to words like treaty, diesel … and other aspects. The whole question of "listening." And then of "silence." The river itself carries a silence that is its own power, which is what it brings to the ocean. So that's what I've learned from writing this poem, finding a language, I don't know if it's the right language, but a language that's allowed me to engage with the river.

Was there any particular language you came up with that was generative?

RITA – There were times when it felt like the poem carried along by itself, if that's what you mean by generative. One word would follow another word and I wouldn't know what that word might be, just trusted it. And then there were other times when it felt kind of tense. The moments with other names, other languages that I'm not fluent in, but that are the river's languages. It taught me how much more I need to learn, and how much I don't know.

FRED – You mean the naming of all the Indigenous Peoples?

RITA – There are lots and lots of names, and their names for the beings, plants, animals, and places. It would be so wonderful to read and/or hear a poem or a story the length of the river completely in Indigenous languages. The different ways of being along the river, and in relationship with the river, that get conveyed and enacted in different languages.

FRED – Could you elaborate on the paradox of learning what you need to learn?

RITA – It relates to the problem of authorship, how it sometimes aggrandizes or idealizes the author as an authority figure. When you are put in that position, you realize how inaccurate that can be if it is played like a god-trick. If the work is doing what I hope it will do, it will encourage people to both listen more carefully, and to voice their own stories and experiences, have more engagement and better relations with the river. To get beyond ego and into deeper relations with land, people, and life. I think the figure of the author can be problematic because of what it makes invisible, so part of the work is to contextualize it so that those social relations and historical relations aren't erased and the importance of collective culture and efforts is better recognized.

My relationship to the watershed is also shaped through the work I've been doing with Dorothy Christian around and with water over the past decade, and knowing that the watershed I'm visiting is her home territory. I want to acknowledge the relationships with people who are in and from that place.

FRED – Could you tell me a little bit more about Dorothy?

RITA – Dorothy is a Secwepemc Okanagan filmmaker, a visual storyteller as she puts it. She's a survivor of the Sixties Scoop too, and deeply dedicated to Indigenous resurgence. I was feeling conscious and thinking of her a lot when we were on our trip. I feel because I was called into this work through that relationship with her that it's important to acknowledge this. She has been and is a very important influence on me, and our water journeys led to the anthology *downstream: reimagining water* that we co-edited to share some of the incredible water work that's being done by so many people in so many different ways.

FRED – If the river is gifting us this language, it's gifting you what you don't know …

RITA – It's reminding me of how much more I still don't know, and to stay humble.

FRED – Is it a reminder of something that's absent?

RITA – Or something I don't have access to, not necessarily absent (though there is that too, of course – the attempted extinguishing of salmon by colonial dams comes to mind for starters). Like when we were at the Ktunaxa band office, there are folks with that knowledge. We don't have it, and I'm not sure that we should have it. There are limits that should be respected. There's a protocol involved in building those relationships. So I think to acknowledge our limits and our positioning is an important thing to do, ethically. I worry that the structures that we're in, under capital, under colonization, tend to oversimplify and misrepresent things that are actually relational. They assume a mindset of access, entitlement, control, when the cultures we need in order to survive on this planet are ones that require we respect and learn from the earth's limits, working to foster the conditions for care, diversity and coexistence of life, rather than a capitalist race to exploit everything to the point of collapse.

As that quote from Bob Perelman that Jeff Derksen uses as an epigraph to his book *Transnational Muscle Cars* (Talonbooks, 2003) says: "… because capitalism makes the nouns / and burns the connections …"

The Maori say: "I am the river, and the river is me." If we understood this more deeply, we would not conduct ourselves in ways that pollute and damage her. The river is a sacred life, and I hope more of us learn this before it is too late.

FRED – Were you consciously avoiding being didactic with the language that you ended up using in your poem?

RITA – No, I wasn't thinking about it. The words that came were the words that came.

FRED – The words that the river gave us and have helped us to receive the river "as is."

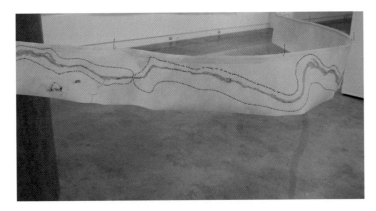

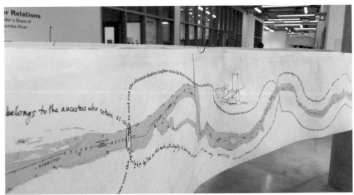

Authors' Acknowledgments

We gratefully acknowledge the Salmon peoples along the entire length of the Columbia River. You are the past, the present, and the future of this river. Thanks to Genevieve Robertson for the cover art, along with Nick Conbere, John Holmgren, Emmy Willis, Zoe Kostuchuk, and Matthew Evenden for their art, participation, and support in *River Relations: A Beholder's Share of the Columbia River.* Particular appreciation for Nick Conbere who coordinates the collaborative project and facilitated the river map that frames the poems. He teaches at Emily Carr University of Art and Design. His past research has explored ways to convey changes in the character of landscapes over time through multilayered narrative artwork.

Thanks to Leslie Smith and Katherine Gillieson for book design and to Charles Simard at Talonbooks for planning and editing. Thanks to Hiromi Goto for photographic companionship. Thanks to Dorothy Christian for the necessary conversations over the years. Dorothy asks, "Can you love the land like I do?" Gratitude also to Eileen Delahanty Pearkes for generous engagement. Hand up to the Wild Salmon Caravan which joyfully teaches us good ways to journey with the river.

Thanks to the **Columbia River** and all her guardians and beholders.

Selected Sources, References, and Influences

Ainsworth Hot Springs (Ainsworth, British Columbia). See http://www.ainsworthhotsprings.com/.

Alexie, Sherman. "The Powwow at the End of the World." In *First Fish, First People: Salmon Tales of the North Pacific Rim*, edited by Judith Roche and Meg McHutchison, 17. Seattle: University of Washington Press; Vancouver: UBC Press, 1998.

Armstrong, Jeannette C. "Water is Siwlkw." In *Water and Indigenous Peoples*, edited by Rutgerd Boelens, Moe Chiba, and Douglas Nakashima, 18–19. Knowledges of Nature 2. Paris: UNESCO, 2006.

Bird, Gloria. "What We Owe." In *The River of History: Prose Poems*. Portland, OR: Trask House Books, 1997.

Blackstock, Michael. "Water: A First Nations' Spiritual and Ecological Perspective." *B.C. Journal of Ecosystems and Management* 1, No. 1 (2001): 1–14. http://forrex .org/sites/default/files/publications/jem_archive/ISS1 /vol1_no1_art7.pdf.

Bolling, David. *How To Save a River: A Handbook for Citizen Action*. Covelo: Island Press, 1994.

Bradford Island Visitor Center at Bonneville Lock and Dam (Cascade Locks, OR). Exhibit panels, 2017. http://www .nwp.usace.army.mil/bonneville/.

Cash, Johnny. "The Rock Island Line." Track 1 on *With His Hot and Blue Guitar*. Sun Records, 1957. Writers unknown. Lyrics at https://genius.com/Johnny-cash -rock-island-line-lyrics.

Christian, Dorothy. "Reconciling with the People and the Land?" In *Cultivating Canada: Reconciliation through the Lens of Cultural Diversity*, edited by Ashok Mathur, Jonathan Dewar, and Mike DeGagné, 69–80. Aboriginal Healing Foundation Research Series. Ottawa: Aboriginal Healing Foundation, 2011.

Christian, Dorothy, and Rita Wong, eds. *downstream: reimagining water*. Environmental Humanities. Waterloo, ON: Wilfrid Laurier University Press, 2016.

Chrystos. *Not Vanishing*. Vancouver, BC: Press Gang, 1989.

Columbia River Inter-Tribal Fish Commission. Accessed 2017–2018. http://www.critfc.org/.

———. *Columbia River Treaty*. Map. October 2014. http:// www.critfc.org/tribal-treaty-fishing-rights/policy -support/columbia-river-treaty/area-blocked-salmon -columbia-basin/.

Columbia Riverkeeper. Accessed 2017–2018. http://columbia riverkeeper.org/.

Confederated Tribes of the Colville Reservation. Accessed 2017–2018. https://www.colvilletribes.com/.

Confluence Project. Accessed 2017–2018. http://www. confluenceproject.org/.

Dam Removal: Science and Decision Making. Washington, DC: H. John Heinz III Center for Science, Economics and the Environment, 2002.

de Leeuw, Sarah. *Skeena*. Halfmoon Bay, BC: Caitlin Press, 2015.

Derksen, Jeff. *Transnational Muscle Cars*. Vancouver, BC: Talonbooks, 2003.

Faith, Karlene, and Kim Pate. "Personal and Political Musings on Activism: A Two-Way Interview." In *An Ideal Prison? Critical Essays on Women's Imprisonment in Canada*, edited by Kelly Hannah-Moffat and Margaret Shaw, 136–147. Halifax: Fernwood Publishing, 2000.

The Friends of Celilo Falls. "The Day the Oregon State Senate Mourned the Flooding of Celilo Falls." YouTube video uploaded February 26, 2014, 35:32. https://friendsofcelilo falls.wordpress.com/2014/02/24/the-day-the-oregon -state-senate-mourned-the-flooding-of-celilo-falls/ and https://www.youtube.com/watch?v=DQBUotzqcWQ.

Gianvito, John, dir. *Profit Motive and the Whispering Wind*. 2007. 58 min.

Goldman, Tom. "Swimming the Columbia River: Man's Journey to Spotlight River's Woes Nears an End." *National Public Radio*, June 26, 2003. http://www.npr .org/templates/story/story.php?storyId=1310820.

Goto, Hiromi. Various photographs.

Harden, Blaine. *A River Lost: The Life and Death of the Columbia*. New York: W. W. Norton & Company, 1996.

Keating, Bob. "Damned and Determined." *Kootenay Mountain Culture* 31 (Summer 2017): 84–93.

Kendall, Linda. "Death of a Community." *BC Studies*, No. 142 /143 (Summer/Autumn 2004): 153–160. http://ojs.library .ubc.ca/index.php/bcstudies/article/view/1722/1768.

Kennedy, Brendan. "I Am the River and the River Is Me: The Implications of a River Receiving Personhood Status." *Cultural Survival Quarterly Magazine* 36, No. 4 (December 2012). https://www.culturalsurvival.org/ publications/cultural-survival-quarterly/i-am-river-and -river-me-implications-river-receiving.

Kinship of Rivers. Accessed March 2017. http://www.kin shipofrivers.org/.

Lakeshore Resort and Campground. Accessed 2017–2018. http://lakeshoreresortcampground.ca/.

Layman, William D. *Native River: The Columbia Remembered*. Seattle, OR: Washington State University Press, 2002.

———. *River of Memory: The Everlasting Columbia*. Wenatchee, WA: Wenatchee Valley Museum & Cultural

Center; Seattle, WA: University of Washington Press; Vancouver, BC: UBC Press, 2006.

The Leap Manifesto. Accessed 2017–2018. https://leap manifesto.org/.

Lippard, Lucy R. *The Lure of the Local: Senses of Place in a Multicentered Society*. New York: The New Press, 1997.

Loo, Tina. "People in the Way: Modernity, Environment, and Society on the Arrow Lakes." *BC Studies*, No. 142 /143 (Summer/Autumn 2004): 161–196. http://ojs.library .ubc.ca/index.php/bcstudies/article/view/1724/1769.

MacAdams, Lewis. *The River*. Santa Cruz, CA: Blue Press, 2007.

Macdonald, Mike. "Artist statement." In *Revisions*, edited by Joane Cardinal-Schubert, Deborah Doxtator, and the Walter Phillips Gallery, 16. Banff, AB: Walter Phillips Gallery, 1992.

Maracle, Lee. "Goodbye Snauq." In Maria Campbell, Tantoo Cardinal, Tomson Highway, Drew Hayden Taylor, Basil Johnston, Thomas King, Brian Maracle, Lee Maracle, Jovette Marchessault, and Rachel Qitsualik, *Our Story: Aboriginal Voices on Canada's Past*, 205–19. Toronto: Anchor Canada, 2005.

———. "Water." In *downstream: reimagining water*, edited by Dorothy Christian and Rita Wong, 33–38. Environmental Humanities. Waterloo, ON: Wilfrid Laurier University Press, 2017.

McAdam (Saysewahum), Sylvia. *Nationhood Interrupted: Revitalizing nêhiyaw Legal Systems*. Vancouver, BC: Purich Publishing, 2015.

Miller, Jay, ed. *Mourning Dove: A Salishan Autobiography*. American Indian Lives series. Lincoln, NE: University of Nebraska Press, 1990.

Nisbet, Jack. *Sources of the River: Tracking David Thompson Across Western North America*. Seattle, OR: Sasquatch Books, 1994.

Pearkes, Eileen. *The Geography of Memory: Recovering Stories of a Landscape's First People*. Winlaw, BC: Kutenai House Press, 2002.

———. *A River Captured: The Columbia River Treaty and Catastrophic Change*. Victoria, BC: Rocky Mountain Books, 2016.

Revelstoke Dam Visitor Centre (Revelstoke, British Columbia). Exhibit panels, 2017. https://www.bchydro.com /community/recreation_areas/visitor-centres/revelstoke -visitor-centre.html.

Sandford, Robert William, Deborah Harford, and Jon O'Riordan. *The Columbia River Treaty: A Primer*. Victoria, BC: Rocky Mountain Books, 2014.

Simpson, Leanne, and Naomi Klein. "Dancing the World into Being: A Conversation with Idle No More's Leanne Simpson." *YES! Magazine*, March 5, 2013. Accessed March 2018. http://www.yesmagazine.org/peace-justice /dancing-the-world-into-being-a-conversation-with -idle-no-more-leanne-simpson.

Sinixt Nation. "Fishing-Recognized Traditional Fishing Areas of the Sinixt People." Accessed March 2018. http:// sinixtnation.org/content/fishing-recognized-traditional -fishing-areas-sinixt-people.

Stafford, William. *The Methow River Poems*. Lewiston, ID: Confluence Press, 1995.

Stewart, Christine. "On Treaty Six from Under Mill Creek Bridge." In *Toward. Some. Air.: Remarks on Poetics of Mad Affect, Militancy, Feminism, Demotic Rhythms, Emptying, Intervention, Reluctance, Indigeneity, Immediacy, Lyric Conceptualism, Commons, Pastoral Margins, Desire, Ambivalence, Disability, The Digital, and Other Practices*, edited by Fred Wah and Amy De'Ath, 133–142. Banff, AB: Banff Centre Press, 2015.

Terbasket, Pauline. "Return of the Salmon." *British Columbia Organic Grower*, July 1, 2016. Accessed March 2018. http:// bcorganicgrower.ca/2016/07/return-of-the-salmon/.

Treehugger. "Guy spends 165 days swimming in Columbia River, has aquatic epiphany." May 20, 2005. https://www .treehugger.com/culture/guy-spends-165-days-swimming -in-columbia-river-has-aquatic-epiphany.html.

U.S. Fish and Wildlife Service. *Lewis and Clark National Wildlife Refuge*. Brochure. November 2009. https:// www.fws.gov/lc/PDF/L&C%20NWR%20General %20Brochure.pdf.

Wanapum Heritage Center (Mattawa, WA). See https:// wanapum.org.

Warshall, Peter. "Watershed Governance: Checklists to Encourage Respect for Waterflows and People." In *Writing on Water*, edited by David Rothenberg and Marta Ulvaeus, 40–57. Cambridge, MA: MIT Press, 2001.

Wilkinson, Myler, and Sutherland, Duff. "'From Our Side We Will Be Good Neighbour[s] to Them': Doukhobor–Sinixt Relations at the Confluence of the Kootenay and Columbia Rivers in the Early Twentieth Century." *BC Studies* 174 (Summer 2012): 33–59. http://ojs.library .ubc.ca/index.php/bcstudies/article/view/2380/183492.

FRED WAH lives in Vancouver and in the West Kootenays. Recent books include *Sentenced to Light*, his collaborations with visual artists, and *is a door*, a series of poems about hybridity. The interactive poem *High Muck a Muck: Playing Chinese* is available online at highmuckamuck.ca. *Scree: The Collected Earlier Poems, 1962–1991* was published by Talonbooks in 2015.

RITA WONG lives and works on unceded Coast Salish territories, also known as Vancouver. Dedicated to questions of water justice, decolonization, and ecology, she is the author of *monkeypuzzle* (Press Gang, 1998), *forage* (Nightwood Editions, 2007), *sybil unrest* (Line Books, 2008, with Larissa Lai), *undercurrent* (Nightwood Editions, 2015), and *perpetual* (Nightwood Editions, 2015, with Cindy Mochizuki), as well as the co-editor of *downstream: reimagining water* (Wilfrid Laurier University Press, 2016, with Dorothy Christian).

Talonbooks
278 East First Avenue, Vancouver, British Columbia, Canada V5T 1A6
talonbooks.com

Talonbooks is located on xʷməθkʷəy̓əm, Sḵwx̱wú7mesh, and səl̓ilwətaʔɫ Lands.

First printing: 2018

Typeset in Minion
Printed and bound in Canada

Interior and cover design by Typesmith
Cover illustrations by Genevieve Robertson
Original map design by Katherine Gillieson and Nick Conbere
Columbia River map design and accompanying sketches by Nick Conbere

Tribes and First Nations of the Columbia River Basin map by Jeremy FiveCrows and used with permission from the Columbia River Inter-Tribal Fish Commission

Talonbooks gratefully acknowledges the financial support of the Canada Council for the Arts, the Government of Canada through the Canada Book Fund, and the Province of British Columbia through the British Columbia Arts Council and the Book Publishing Tax Credit.

LIBRARY AND ARCHIVES CANADA CATALOGUING IN PUBLICATION

Wong, Rita, 1968–, author
    Beholden : a poem as long as the river / Rita Wong
& Fred Wah.

Columbia River map design and accompanying sketches
    by Nick Conbere.
Includes bibliographical references.

ISBN 978-1-77201-211-8 (SOFTCOVER)

    1. Columbia River – Poetry. I. Wah, Fred, 1939–, author
II. Conbere, Nick, illustrator III. Title.

PS8595.O5975 B44 2018   C811ʹ.54   C2018-905736-X

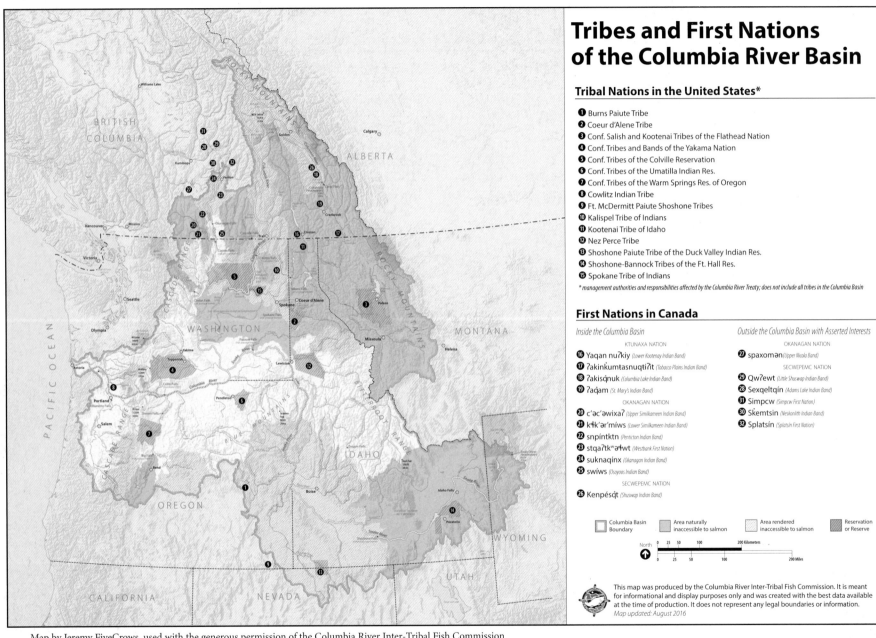

Tribes and First Nations of the Columbia River Basin

Tribal Nations in the United States*

1. Burns Paiute Tribe
2. Coeur d'Alene Tribe
3. Conf. Salish and Kootenai Tribes of the Flathead Nation
4. Conf. Tribes and Bands of the Yakama Nation
5. Conf. Tribes of the Colville Reservation
6. Conf. Tribes of the Umatilla Indian Res.
7. Conf. Tribes of the Warm Springs Res. of Oregon
8. Cowlitz Indian Tribe
9. Ft. McDermitt Paiute Shoshone Tribes
10. Kalispel Tribe of Indians
11. Kootenai Tribe of Idaho
12. Nez Perce Tribe
13. Shoshone Paiute Tribe of the Duck Valley Indian Res.
14. Shoshone-Bannock Tribes of the Ft. Hall Res.
15. Spokane Tribe of Indians

management authorities and responsibilities affected by the Columbia River Treaty; does not include all tribes in the Columbia Basin

First Nations in Canada

Inside the Columbia Basin

KTUNAXA NATION

16. Yaqan nuʔkiy (Lower Kootenay Indian Band)
17. ʔakinḱumȼasnuqtiʔit (Tobacco Plains Indian Band)
18. ʔakisq́nuk (Columbia Lake Indian Band)
19. ʔaq̓am (St. Mary's Indian Band)

OKANAGAN NATION

20. c'əc'əwixaʔ (Upper Similkameen Indian Band)
21. kɬk'ər'míws (Lower Similkameen Indian Band)
22. snpíntktn (Penticton Indian Band)
23. stqaʔtk"əɬwt (Westbank First Nation)
24. suknaqínx (Okanagan Indian Band)
25. swíws (Osoyoos Indian Band)

SECWEPEMC NATION

26. Kenpésq̓t (Shuswap Indian Band)

Outside the Columbia Basin with Asserted Interests

OKANAGAN NATION

27. spaxomən (Upper Nicola Band)

SECWEPEMC NATION

29. Qwʔewt (Little Shuswap Indian Band)
28. Sexqeltqín (Adams Lake Indian Band)
31. Simpcw (Simpcw First Nation)
30. Sḱemtsín (Neskonlith Indian Band)
32. Splatsín (Splatsín First Nation)

Legend:
- Columbia Basin Boundary
- Area naturally inaccessible to salmon
- Area rendered inaccessible to salmon
- Reservation or Reserve

North

0 25 50 100 200 Kilometers
0 25 50 100 200 Miles

This map was produced by the Columbia River Inter-Tribal Fish Commission. It is meant for informational and display purposes only and was created with the best data available at the time of production. It does not represent any legal boundaries or information.
Map updated: August 2016

Map by Jeremy FiveCrows, used with the generous permission of the Columbia River Inter-Tribal Fish Commission